W9-BJN-529

SECOND EDITION

WORKBOOK FOR

HARMONIC PRACTICE

IN TONAL MUSIC

W · W · NORTON & COMPANY · NEW YORK · LONDON

SECOND EDITION

WORKBOOK FOR
HARMONIC PRACTICE
IN TONAL MUSIC

Robert Gauldin

PROFESSOR EMERITUS OF MUSIC THEORY
EASTMAN SCHOOL OF MUSIC

CREDITS

Coltrane, "Giant Steps" (p. 372): Used by permission of Jowcol Music.

Crumb, *Makrokosmos I* (p. 30): Copyright © 1974 by C. F. Peters Corporation. Used by permission. All rights reserved.

Desmond, "Take Five" (p. 173): Copyright © 1960, 1988 Desmond Music Company (U.S.A.) and Desmond Music Company (World except U.S.A.). Used with permission.

Elgar, Variations on an Original Theme 'Enigma,' Op. 36 (p. 279): Copyright © 1899 Novello & Company Limited, 8/9 Frith Street, London WID 3JB, England. International Copyright Secured. All Rights Reserved. Used by permission.

Gershwin, "Nice Work if You Can Get It" (p. 334): By George and Ira Gershwin. © 1937 (Renewed) George Gershwin Music and Ira Gershwin Music. All rights administered by WB Music Corp. All Rights Reserved. Used by Permission. WARNER BROS. PUBLICATIONS U.S. INC., Miami, FL 33014.

Henderson, "Five Foot Two, Eyes of Blue (Has Anybody Seen my Girl?)" (p. 182): Words by Joe Young and Sam Lewis. Music by Ray Henderson. © 1925 LEO FEIST, INC. © Renewed 1953 WAROCK CORP., LEO FEIST, INC., AND HENDERSON MUSIC CO. Used by Permission of Henderson Music Co. All rights reserved.

Henderson, "The Birth of the Blues" (p. 344): © 1925 LEO FEIST, INC. © Renewed 1953 WAROCK CORP., LEO FEIST, INC., AND HENDERSON MUSIC CO. Used by Permission of Henderson Music Co. All rights reserved. Used by Permission of Henderson Music Co. © 1926 (Renewed) Warner Bros. Inc. Rights for extended Renewal Term in the U.S. controlled by Warner Bros. Inc., Ray Henderson Music and Staphen Ballentine Music. All rights outside the U.U. controlled by Warner Bros. Inc. All Rights Reserved. Used by Permission. WARNER BROS. PUBLICATIONS U.S. INC., Miami, FL 33014.

Kern, "The Way You Look Tonight" (p. 324): By Dorothy Fields and Jerome Kern. © 1936 (Renewed) Universal – PolyGram International Publishing, Inc. and Aldi Music Co. All Rights Reserved. Used by Permission. WARNER BROS. PUBLICATIONS U.S. INC., Miami, FL 33014.

Stravinsky, *Le Sacre du Printemps* (p. 89): © Copyright 1912, 1921 by Hawkes & Son (London) Ltd.; Copyright Renewed. Reprinted by permission of Boosey & Hawkes, Inc.

The Publisher has made every effort to contact all copyright holders. If proper acknowledgment has not been made, we ask to be contacted.

Copyright © 2004, 1997 by W. W. Norton & Company, Inc.

All rights reserved.
Printed in the United States of America
Second Edition

The text of this book is composed in New Caledonia.
Composition by A-R Editions, Inc.
Manufacturing by Courier, Westford.
Book Designer: Paul Lacy

ISBN 0-393-97667-X (pbk.)

W. W. Norton & Company, Inc., 500 Fifth Avenue, New York, NY 10110
www.wwnorton.com

W. W. Norton & Company Ltd., Castle House, 75/76 Wells Street, London WIT 3QT

6 7 8 9 0

W. W. Norton & Company has been independent since its founding in 1923, when William Warder Norton and Mary D. Herter Norton first published lectures delivered at the People's Institute, the adult education division of New York City's Cooper Union. The Nortons soon expanded their program beyond the Institute, publishing books by celebrated academics from America and abroad. By mid-century, the two major pillars of Norton's publishing program—trade books and college texts—were firmly established. In the 1950s, the Norton family transferred control of the company to its employees, and today—with a staff of four hundred and a comparable number of trade, college, and professional titles published each year—W. W. Norton & Company stands as the largest and oldest publishing house owned wholly by its employees.

CONTENTS*

PREFACE ix

PART ONE: THE BASIC ELEMENTS OF MUSIC

CHAPTER 1: Pitch and Intervals 1

CHAPTER 2: Rhythm and Meter I: BEAT, METER, AND RHYTHMIC NOTATION 11

CHAPTER 3: Tonic, Scale, and Melody 17

CHAPTER 4: Triads and Seventh Chords 27

CHAPTER 5: Musical Texture and Chordal Spacing 35

CHAPTER 6: Partwriting in Four-Voice Texture 43

CHAPTER 7: Melodic Figuration and Dissonance I: EMBELLISHING TONES 47

PART TWO: DIATONIC HARMONY

CHAPTER 9: The Primary Triads: TONIC, DOMINANT, AND SUBDOMINANT CHORDS 57

CHAPTER 10: The Dominant Seventh: EMBELLISHING THE TONIC HARMONY 65

CHAPTER 11: The Tonic and Subdominant Chords in First Inversion: THE I⁶ AND IV⁶ AS EMBELLISHING CHORDS 77

CHAPTER 12: Phrase Structure and Grouping 85

CHAPTER 13: Linear Dominants: V⁶, VII°⁶, AND INVERSIONS OF V⁷ 93

CHAPTER 14: The Pre-Dominant II and II⁷ Chords 105

CHAPTER 15: Melodic Figuration and Dissonance II: SUSPENSIONS AND OTHER EMBELLISHING TONES 117

CHAPTER 16: The $\frac{6}{4}$ and Other Linear Chords 127

CHAPTER 17: The VI, III, and Other Diatonic Triads 137

* **Note:** Workbook exercises and keyboard exercises do not appear for all chapters or sections in the textbook. Specifically, no Workbook exercises appear for Chapters 8 and 42, as well as Appendixes 1, 2, 4, 5, and 6. No keyboard exercises appear for Chapters 2, 6, 7, 8, 12, 18, 24, 25, 26, 31, 33, 36, 38, 42, and Appendixes 1 through 6.

CHAPTER 18: Rhythm and Meter II: RHYTHMIC DEVIATIONS AND METRICAL DISSONANCE   147

CHAPTER 19: The Leading-Tone Seventh Chord and Other Seventh Chords   153

CHAPTER 20: Harmonic Sequences I: TRIADIC ROOT MOVEMENT BY 5TH, 2ND, AND 3RD   165

CHAPTER 21: Tonicization and Modulation I: SECONDARY DOMINANT CHORDS   175

CHAPTER 22: Tonicization and Modulation II: MODULATION TO V AND III   185

CHAPTER 23: Harmonic Sequences II: SEQUENCES OF SEVENTH CHORDS AND OTHER SEQUENCES   195

CHAPTER 24: Simple Forms   205

CHAPTER 25: Two Analysis Projects   233

PART THREE: CHROMATIC HARMONY

CHAPTER 26: Review of Diatonic Harmony   241

CHAPTER 27: Tonicization and Modulation III: MODULATION TO CLOSELY RELATED KEYS   245

CHAPTER 28: Modal Exchange and Mixture Chords   255

CHAPTER 29: The Neapolitan Chord   265

CHAPTER 30: Augmented Sixth Chords   275

CHAPTER 31: Complex Forms   285

CHAPTER 32: Embellishing Chromatic Chords   303

CHAPTER 33: Dominant Prolongation   313

CHAPTER 34: Modulation to Foreign Keys I   319

CHAPTER 35: Ninth, Eleventh, Thirteenth, and Added-Note Chords   327

CHAPTER 36: Implication and Realization   335

CHAPTER 37: Harmonic Sequences III: CHROMATIC ELABORATIONS OF DIATONIC SEQUENCES   339

CHAPTER 38: An Analysis Project   347

PART FOUR: ADVANCED CHROMATIC TECHNIQUES

CHAPTER 39: Chromatic Voice Leading   353

CHAPTER 40: Modulation to Foreign Keys II   359

CHAPTER 41: Symmetical Divisions of the Octave   369

APPENDIX 3: An Introduction to Species Counterpoint   379

KEYBOARD EXERCISES

CHAPTER 1: Pitch and Intervals   383

CHAPTER 3: Tonic, Scale, and Melody   386

CHAPTER 4: Triads and Seventh Chords   387

CHAPTER 5: Musical Texture and Chordal Spacing   389

CHAPTER 9: The Primary Triads: TONIC, DOMINANT, AND SUBDOMINANT CHORDS   392

CHAPTER 10: The Dominant Seventh: EMBELLISHING THE TONIC HARMONY   395

CHAPTER 11: The Tonic and Subdominant Chords in First Inversion: THE I⁶ AND IV⁶ AS EMBELLISHING CHORDS   398

CHAPTER 13: Linear Dominants: V⁶, VII°⁶, AND INVERSIONS OF V⁷   401

CHAPTER 14: The Pre-Dominant II and II⁷ Chords   404

CHAPTER 15: Melodic Figuration and Dissonance II: SUSPENSIONS AND OTHER EMBELLISHING TONES   408

CHAPTER 16: The $\frac{6}{4}$ and Other Linear Chords   411

CHAPTER 17: The VI, III, and Other Diatonic Triads   414

CHAPTER 19: The Leading-Tone Seventh Chord and Other Seventh Chords   417

CHAPTER 20: Harmonic Sequences I: TRIADIC ROOT MOVEMENT BY 5TH, 2ND, AND 3RD   420

CHAPTER 21: Tonicization and Modulation I: SECONDARY DOMINANT CHORDS   423

CHAPTER 22: Tonicization and Modulation II: MODULATION TO Ⅴ AND Ⅲ   427

CHAPTER 23: Harmonic Sequences II: SEQUENCES OF SEVENTH CHORDS AND OTHER SEQUENCES   430

CHAPTER 27: Tonicization and Modulation III: MODULATION TO CLOSELY RELATED KEYS   433

CHAPTER 28: Modal Exchange and Mixture Chords   437

CHAPTER 29: The Neapolitan Chord   440

CHAPTER 30: Augmented Sixth Chords   442

CHAPTER 32: Embellishing Chromatic Chords   445

CHAPTER 34: Modulation to Foreign Keys I   448

CHAPTER 35: Ninth, Eleventh, Thirteenth, and Added-Note Chords   450

CHAPTER 37: Harmonic Sequences III: CHROMATIC ELABORATIONS OF DIATONIC
SEQUENCES   452

CHAPTER 39: Chromatic Voice Leading   455

CHAPTER 40: Modulation to Foreign Keys II   457

CHAPTER 41: Symmetrical Divisions of the Octave   459

P R E F A C E

This Workbook to accompany the Second Edition of *Harmonic Practice in Tonal Music* provides students with a wide variety of written assignments and keyboard exercises. By working through them, as well as the textbook's review self-quizzes, students will gain a firm grasp of the concepts and procedures presented in the text. Reflecting the revisions made in the Second Edition of the textbook, exercises have been added throughout the Workbook, reinforcing the fundamental concepts of each chapter (especially the early chapters). The supplemental drills at the beginning of many of the harmony chapters focus on chord-spelling and creating short progressions that stress typical ways of approaching and departing from specific chords. In addition to an appended list of compositions for analysis, Chapters 24 and 31 now contain complete movements, recordings of which are included on the *Harmonic Practice in Tonal Music* CD-ROM.

THE WORKBOOK EXERCISES

The Workbook assignments include a broad range of written drills: short harmonic models to complete, figured-bass exercises (some of which are not supplied with figured-bass numbers), melodies for harmonization, sequence-completion, original composition projects, and excerpts for analysis. Comments and questions accompanying the analytical assignments provide potential topics for class discussion. For those chapters focusing on specific chord functions, the Second Edition includes supplemental assignments at the beginning of the chapter, which emphasize chord-spelling and short, three-to-five note progressions to complete or analyze.

Although the number of assignments is sufficient to cover the main points of each chapter, the instructor should feel free to create additional exercises or delete those that seem redundant, as the need arises. In addition, the Workbook's written assignments and keyboard exercises should be accompanied by an aural skills program that embraces sight-singing and melodic dictation.

With the exception of those excerpts marked with a special "CD" icon ( ), note that the analytical passages from music literature appearing in this Workbook are *not* recorded on the accompanying CD-ROM. Therefore, students are encouraged to acquaint themselves with these passages at the keyboard, which provides the best possible method of absorbing the sound and structure of theoretical elements and concepts.

THE KEYBOARD EXERCISES

The keyboard exercises serve as an intermediary step between the written assignments and ear-training drills, providing a more practical, performance-oriented approach to theory. They reflect the written assignments found in the Workbook and therefore should be used in conjunction with them.

These exercises will familiarize the student with the sounds of the various intervals, chords, and harmonic progressions in tonal music. Although primary emphasis is placed on playing chords and harmonic progressions at the piano, the student should also keep in mind the melodic characteristics of the soprano and bass voices, heard both separately and in combination.

Located in the final section of this Workbook, the keyboard exercises are arranged by chapter; note that no exercises have been included for those chapters that do not require keyboard reinforcement.

Most of these exercises are not difficult to play from a technical standpoint—especially those in the early chapters. Usually, the "problem" is *what* to play (a function of the mind), rather than *how* to play it (a function of the fingers).

THE BASIC ELEMENTS OF MUSIC

C H A P T E R   1

Pitch and Intervals

1 Identify the following pitches on the staff with their correct octave designation. Use the top space for those in the treble clef and the bottom space for those in the bass clef; the first example is completed for you.[1]

Example 1.1

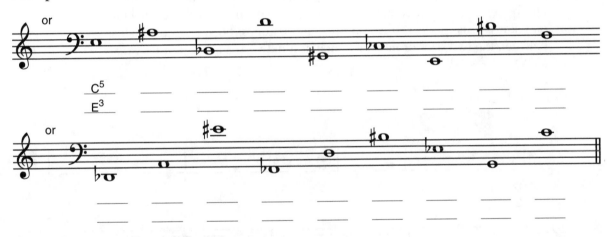

2 **A.** Write the indicated pitch on the staff, making sure that it is in the correct register. Note the changes of clefs.

Example 1.2A

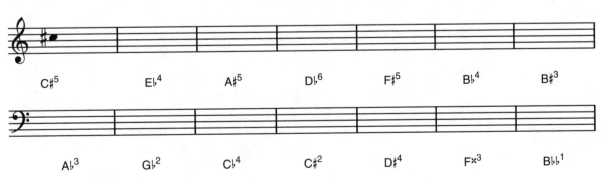

1. This same exercise may be used with the alto and tenor clefs as well.

B. To the right of each pitch, write its enharmonic as in the first model. Then identify both pitches in their correct register.

Example 1.2B

3 A series of harmonic intervals using white-note or natural pitches are given below.

A. Identify each diatonic interval with its proper abbreviation and indicate the number of half steps it contains. The first group of simple intervals includes only 2nds, 3rds, perfect 4ths and 5ths, and tritones; be sure to distinguish between the two sizes of intervals, such as a m2 versus a M2 or a P4 versus an A4.

Example 1.3A

B. This group of diatonic intervals is made up of 6ths, 7ths, and octaves. Do
the same as in Example 1.3A.

Example 1.3B

4   First identify each white-note diatonic interval. Then write out its inversion on
the staff and identify it as well, as in the model.

Example 1.4

5   Compare the white-note harmonic interval between each black notehead and
the sustained white note, and then indicate above the staff whether the interval
is consonant (C) or dissonant (D). We will assume that all perfect 4ths and
tritones are dissonant.

Example 1.5

The remaining exercises involve spelling intervals with various accidentals. We will begin with major and minor 2nds and gradually introduce the other intervals in the following order: perfect 5ths and perfect 4ths, major and minor 3rds, major and minor 6ths, major and minor 7ths, and finally various diminished and augmented intervals.

6 Write the indicated succession of melodic major and minor 2nds. Do not substitute an augmented prime (such as C–C♯) for a minor 2nd (C–D♭). Your concluding pitch should be D⁴, as given.

Remember that the natural major 2nds are C–D, D–E, F–G, G–A, and A–B. When spelling any major 2nd involving these pitch classes, both notes will carry the same accidental. To spell a minor 2nd involving these pitch classes, the size will have to be reduced by one half step, using an appropriate accidental. The natural minor 2nds are E–F and B–C. When spelling any minor 2nd involving these pitch classes, both notes will carry the same accidental, whereas to spell a major 2nd involving these pitch classes, the size will have to be increased by one half step, using an appropriate accidental.

Example 1.6

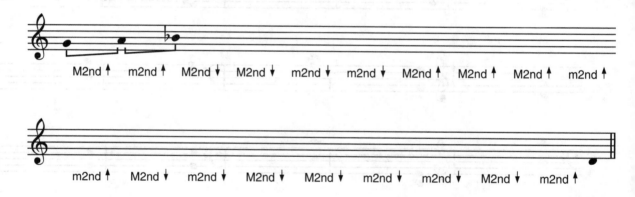

7 Identify the type of interval (M2 or m2) in the provided space.

Example 1.7

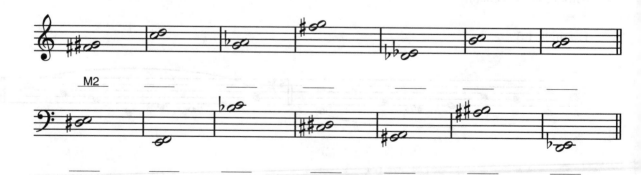

8 Study the succession of intervals in the opening measure. Then continue this pattern in strict fashion to the final note, which should be C♯⁶, as given.

Remember that the natural perfect 5ths and 4ths are C–G, D–A, E–B, F–C, G–D, and A–E. When spelling any perfect 5th or perfect 4th involving these pitch classes, both notes will carry the same accidental. Since B–F is a tritone, when spelling a perfect 5th involving these pitch classes, the B–F, a diminished 5th, will have to be increased by one half step, using an appropriate accidental. When spelling a perfect 4th involving these pitch classes, the F–B, an augmented 4th, will have to be decreased by one half step, using an appropriate accidental.

Example 1.8

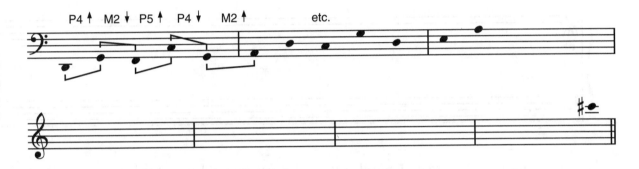

9 The two melodic passages below employ only major and minor 2nds, perfect 5ths, and perfect 4ths. Identify each interval in the provided spaces.

Example 1.9

10 Using only minor and major 3rds, not augmented 2nds or diminished 4ths, build an ascending succession of melodic 3rds above the given C^2 so that it contains all twelve pitch classes with no enharmonic duplications. You may wish to work out your solution on another sheet and then copy the results here.

Remember that the natural major 3rds are C–E, F–A, and G–B. When spelling any major 3rd involving these pitch classes, both notes will carry the same accidental. When spelling any minor 3rd involving these pitch classes, the size of the interval will have to be decreased by one half step, using the appropriate accidental. The natural minor 3rds are D–F, E–G, A–C, and B–D. When spelling minor 3rds, simply reverse the process cited above.

Example 1.10

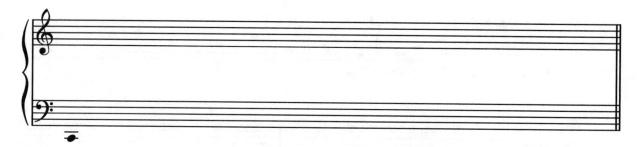

Can you figure out some interval pattern that would avoid an extended trial-and-error approach?

11 Example 1.11

A. Circle only the major 3rds.

B. Circle only the minor 3rds.

12 Write out the continuation of the descending stepwise white notes, using the pattern of major and minor 2nds established in the first two measures. Next, analyze the harmonic intervals in the first measure, and continue their pattern in the succeeding measures.

Example 1.12

13 The following series of harmonic 6ths occurs in Chopin's "Double-Sixth" Etude, Op. 25, No. 8. Denote the type of 6th (major or minor) below the staff. Do you see any recurring patterns? If so, bracket them.

Remember that sixths are simply inverted thirds: the minor 6th is the inversion of the major 3rd, and the major 6th is the inversion of the minor 3rd. In spelling a minor 6th, think of the pitch classes of a major 3rd; in spelling a major 6th, think of the pitch classes of a minor 3rd.

Example 1.13

14 Example 1.14

A. Write the designated type of sixth (major or minor) below the given notes.

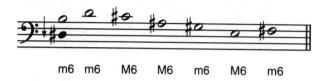

m6   m6   M6   M6   m6   M6   m6

B. Write the designated type of sixth (major or minor) above the given notes.

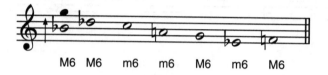

M6   M6   m6   m6   M6   m6   M6

15 Example 1.15

A. Circle all examples of harmonic minor 7ths.

B. Circle all examples of harmonic major 7ths.

Remember that sevenths are inverted seconds. The minor 7th is the inversion of the major 2nd, and the major 7th is the inversion of the minor 2nd. In spelling a minor 7th, think of the pitch classes of a major 2nd; in spelling a major 7th, think of the pitch classes of a minor 2nd.

16 The following set of pitches appears in Alban Berg's *Lyric Suite*.

A. Analyze each successive melodic interval in the space provided. The first two are done for you.

Example 1.16A

m2 ↓   m6 ↑   ___   ___   ___   ___   ___   ___   ___   ___

What do you notice about the number of different pitch classes and different simple intervals?

_____

_____

B. Now reverse the direction of each interval by writing its exact inverted or mirrored form (see the first three notes).

Example 1.16B

(m2 ↑   m6 ↓)

Where do your first six pitches occur in the original set?

_____

Where do your last six pitches occur in the original set?

_____

_____

17 Write the indicated diminished or augmented intervals above and below the given tones. Do not use enharmonic spellings.

Example 1.17

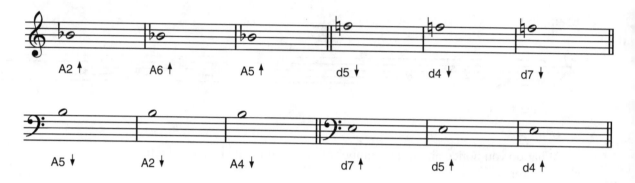

18 Identify the given harmonic interval and specify the number of half steps it contains. Then write its inverted form (perfect 5th = perfect 4th, etc.) and specify the number of half steps it contains. The first example is done for you.

Example 1.18

19 As a class, try making a catalogue of tunes that begin with the various melodic intervals, both ascending and descending. For instance, "The Star Spangled Banner" opens with a descending minor 3rd. For which intervals do you expect to have trouble finding appropriate tunes?

CHAPTER 2

Rhythm and Meter I:

BEAT, METER, AND RHYTHMIC NOTATION

1 Play or listen to the following passage on the CD-ROM. Now list those elements that contribute to the impression of duple meter.

_____

_____

_____

Example 2.1

SCHUBERT: MARCHE MILITAIRE, OP. 51, NO. 1

2 Choose one of the metrical situations listed below and compose an original melody about eight measures long for a solo woodwind instrument. The choice of pitches for your melody is up to you, but your piece should convey one of the meters or the lack of it listed below. Perform your piece in class to see if your fellow students agree.

   a. Compound duple meter
   b. Simple triple meter
   c. Compound quadruple meter
   d. Regular beat but no sense of one prevailing meter
   e. No regular beat (or even a sense of beat)

Example 2.2

3 Supply the following meter signatures, using the format given in the first
   example. In all cases assume a moderate to fast tempo.

Example 2.3

$\frac{2}{4}$ = 2♩   ¢ =

$\frac{9}{4}$ = $\frac{6}{8}$ =

$\frac{12}{16}$ = $\frac{9}{8}$ =

$\frac{3}{4}$ =

4 A. Beam the following succession of eighth notes to correspond to metrical
      groupings in $\frac{3}{4}$ and $\frac{6}{8}$, converting all tied notes into appropriate large note
      values.

Example 2.4A

$\frac{3}{4}$ | | | | ‖

$\frac{6}{8}$ | | | | ‖

B. Regroup the following series of note values into measures of either $\frac{3}{2}$ or $\frac{4}{2}$, keeping the notes in the same order that is given. You may have to break up some of the note values if they tie over into the next bar.

Example 2.4B

$\frac{3}{2}$ 𝅗𝅥 |

$\frac{4}{2}$ 𝅗𝅥 |

Does this rhythmical succession suggest triple or quadruple meter?

_____

Where do the barlines in the two examples synchronize or align themselves?

_____

Can you give a reason for this?

_____

5 Supply a meter signature that is appropriate for the rhythmic grouping in each measure below. In some cases, more than one signature is possible; see the first example.

Example 2.5

6 Circle the notational errors in the following three rhythmic passages. There are a total of eight errors.

Example 2.6

A.

B.

C.

7 As an exercise in transferring music accurately, carefully copy the first three pairs of staves from the following example to the staves that are provided. Strive to reproduce every single mark as faithfully as possible. Completing this example will help you become more proficient in notating and copying music, a task you will be called upon to do in many of the examples in this workbook.

Example 2.7

SCHUMANN: "★★★" FROM *ALBUM FOR THE YOUNG*, OP. 68, NO. 21

8 Do a melodic analysis of the three tunes provided below, similar to those found
at the end of Chapter 3 in the text. Be sure to include the key, phrase lengths,
framing scale degrees of each phrase, and any other long-range melodic
characteristics you may note.

Examples 3.8A and B

A. "SIMPLE GIFTS" (SHAKER TUNE)

B. "JEUNE FILLETTE" (FRENCH FOLK SONG)

Example 3.8C

Example 3.8C

C. BRAHMS: SYMPHONY NO. 1 IN C MINOR, IV

Many writers have remarked on the striking similarity between Beethoven's "Ode to Joy" melody, found in Chapter 3 of the text, and the principal theme of the last movement of Brahms's Symphony No. 1 in C Minor. What similarities do you notice between the two?

_____

_____

9 Compose two four-measure melodic phrases in the staves provided. For each, incorporate the following characteristics:

A. Treble clef, minor mode, simple triple meter, and an inconclusive cadence.

Example 3.9A

B. Bass clef, major mode, compound duple meter, and a conclusive cadence.

Example 3.9B

CHAPTER 6

Partwriting in Four-Voice Texture

1 These four-voice progressions contain various types of partwriting and spelling errors; assume the figured bass are correct. Circle and identify the specific problem in each example.

Example 6.1

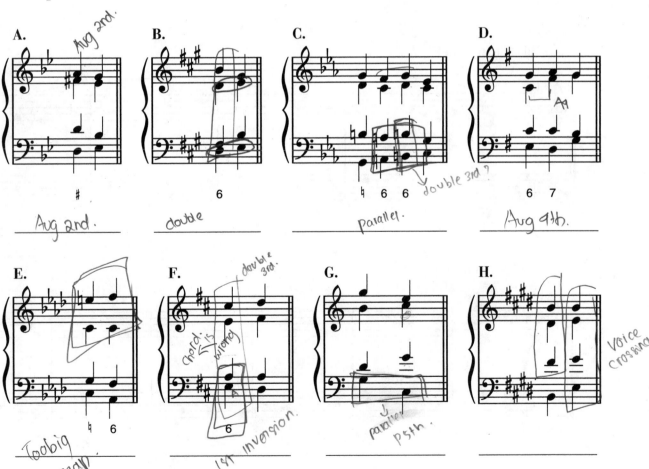

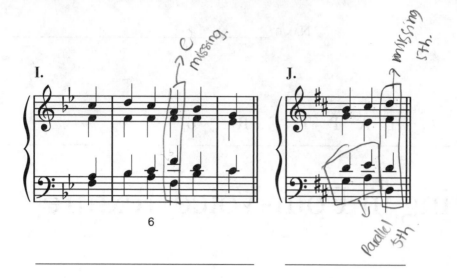

I.   6

J.

2   Using the indicated chord structures above the staff and the figured-bass symbols below the staff, fill in the alto and tenor voices to create a four-voice texture. Employ the doublings listed earlier in the preceding chapter, unless otherwise instructed.

Example 6.2

A.   (all close structure)

B.   (all open structure)

NAME   Priscilla Clara

CHAPTER   7

Melodic Figuration and Dissonance I:

EMBELLISHING TONES

1 The circled note in each of the following three-note figures is either a consonant embellishing chord tone or a dissonant non-harmonic tone. If it is a chord tone, write C above it. If it is a non-harmonic tone, identify its melodic type, using the following abbreviations: P for passing tone, N for neighboring tone, A for anticipation, IN for incomplete neighbor, S for suspension, along with the prefix A for accented—for instance, AP for accented passing tone.

Example 7.1

2 The passages in Example 7.2 contain dissonant embellishing tones that are circled in the music. Identify each melodic type on the score, using the above abbreviations.

Example 7.2

A.

B.

C.

3 The following excerpts from music literature likewise make use of various dissonant embellishing tones, which are circled. Again, identify each and then answer the accompanying questions.

Example 7.3

A. ANDREA GABRIELI: KYRIE FROM *MISSA BREVIS*

B. HAYDN: PIANO SONATA IN C MAJOR, HOB. XVI, NO. 35, III

C. Bach: Fugue in E Major from *The Well-Tempered Clavier*, Book II

D. "O Haupt voll Blut und Wunden" (modified Bach harmonization)

E. Beethoven: Piano Concerto No. 1 in C Major, Op. 15, I

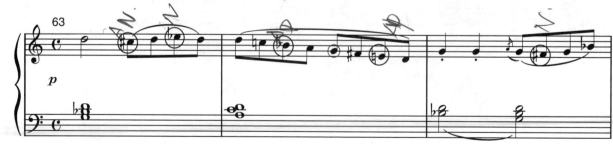

Do any of the excerpts contain melodic dissonances that fall into only one category, such as unaccented stepwise, accented leaping, and so forth? If so, list those excerpts by letter in the space below, and indicate the specific category.

_____

_____

4 Recopy the following piece, using the method of nonharmonic reduction found in Chapter 7 of the text. Use stemmed and unstemmed noteheads and connecting slurs, and identify each embellishing tone with its proper abbreviation. The first measure is done for you.

Example 7.4

5 Recopy the four passages below, adding appropriate embellishing tones in each
   example as follows:

   A. Only unaccented passing tones in any voice. Be careful, for in one measure
      the addition of a passing tone may create parallel 5ths with the tenor.

   Example 7.5A

B. Only unaccented/stepwise tones (P, N, A) in any voice.

Example 7.5B

C. Only suspensions in the indicated voices.

Example 7.5C

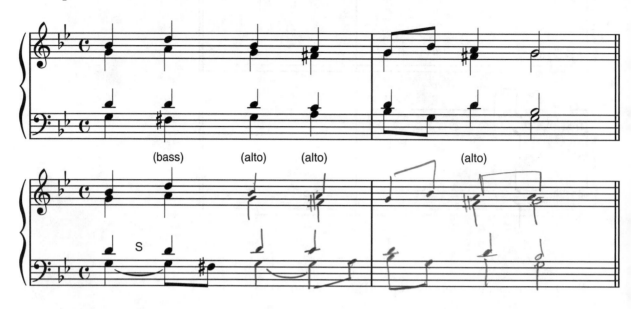

D. Only accented/stepwise tones (AP or AN) in any voice.

Example 7.5D

DIATONIC

HARMONY

E.

F.

6 Realize the following figured-bass exercises in four-voice texture by filling in the alto and tenor and providing a Roman numeral analysis. All embellishing tones are circled. The structure of the first triad as well as an occasional interior triad is provided. In some exercises you can retain the same chord structure throughout; in others you may have to change the structure occasionally.

Example 9.6

A.

B.

C.

D.

E.

7 Harmonize the two tunes below in four-voice texture, using only root-position I, IV, and V triads. Both consist of two short phrases, as denoted by the slurs. First sketch in a plausible Roman numeral analysis and bass line, taking into account any possible passing or neighboring tones. Then add the remaining inner voices. The rate of chord change is relatively slow in these tunes. When the melody leaps to a different chord tone within the same harmony, you may either retain or change the chord structure, as discussed in Chapter 5.

Example 9.7

A.

e:

B.

B♭:

8 Below each of the following passages provide a Roman numeral analysis and circle any dissonant embellishing tones in the music. Then in the empty staves write out a voice-leading reduction (soprano and bass voices only). Each essential note should be stemmed. The last two examples consist of two short phrases.

Example 9.8

A.

e:

B.

Bb:

C.

a:

Example 10.3

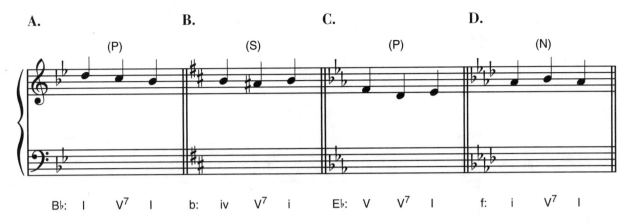

Bb: I V⁷ I   b: iv V⁷ i   Eb: V V⁷ I   f: i V⁷ I

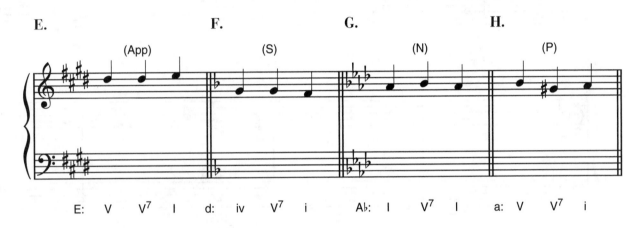

E: V V⁷ I   d: iv V⁷ i   Ab: I V⁷ I   a: V V⁷ i

4 The passage below contains a number of various partwriting errors, such as incorrect doubling, structure, spelling, parallels, and treatment of a V⁷. Circle each error and number it on the music. Then copy the number in the space provided below and indicate the nature of the error.

Example 10.4

_____

_____

_____

_____

5   Realize the following figured-bass exercises in four-part texture and provide a Roman numeral analysis. Enclose all *embellishing* Vs and V⁷s in parentheses and indicate the treatment of each chordal 7th, using the abbreviations in Example 10.2. Several of the phrases contain circled embellishing tones.

Example 10.5A

A.

Example 10.5B features a sustained bass pedal on the tonic, which imports a serene lullaby character to the passage; use the *downward stemmed notes* above the low E as the basis of your figured bass.

Example 10.5B

B.

Example 10.5C

C.

Since Example 10.5D has an unfigured bass, you will have to deduce what the chords should be from the outer voices.

Example 10.5D

D.

Provide a soprano line in Example 10.5E. Since the bass line repeats, provide a *different* upper voice for the last four measures.

Example 10.5E

E.

Gb:

6 Many short musical genres, such as marches, waltzes, rags, polkas, and character pieces, share a stereotypical harmonic scheme. The melody to the Trio of the march *Under the Double Eagle* appears in Example 10.6. Scan this tune and indicate with Roman numerals the implied chords you would use to harmonize it: I, IV, V, or V⁷. Notice that the harmonies do not always change with the phrasing indicated by the slurs. The chord progression on which this Trio is based also appears in the turn-of-the-century waltz *Over the Waves,* and is very similar to the progression in the opening section of Johann Strauss's *The Beautiful Blue Danube.*

Example 10.6

Eb:

7 Harmonize the two melodies in Example 10.7 in four-voice texture, using only I, IV, V, and V⁷ chords. Always consider the harmonic rhythm, or the rate at which the harmonies change. You may wish to elaborate your bass line and inner voices with a few embellishing passing or neighboring tones, but be careful not to create parallel 5ths.

Example 10.7

A.

A:

B.

b♭:

8 The following three excerpts employ only tonic and dominant harmonies (I, V, and V^7). Add a Roman numeral analysis below the music; enclose all embellishing chords in parentheses and circle all dissonant embellishing tones. Write out a voice-leading reduction in the empty staves provided, remembering that essential harmonies are stemmed and embellishing harmonies remain unstemmed.

    A. In this Bach passage treat the upper voices as a compound melody, as shown in the first chord.

Example 10.8A

BACH: *Brandenburg Concerto* No. 4 in G Major, III (simplified)

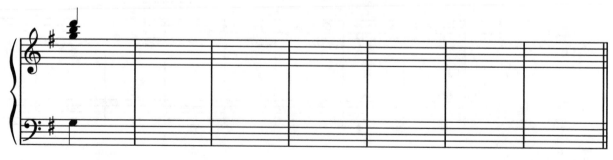

G:

B. Consider this excerpt as a single eight-measure phrase. Do you find any similarity between this Haydn passage and the one we discussed in Examples 10.13 and 10.14? If so, in what way?

Example 10.8B

HAYDN: SYMPHONY NO. 97 IN C MAJOR, III, TRIO

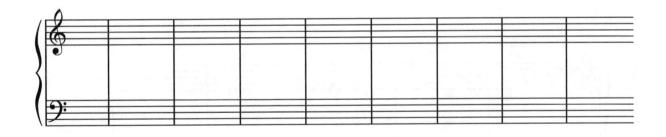

C. Take note of the frequent embellishing tones in the following melody. Several have been circled in measures 3 and 4.

Example 10.8C

CHOPIN: ETUDE IN E MAJOR, OP. 10, NO. 3

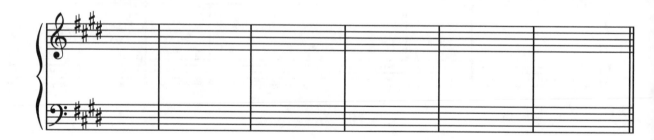

9   Provide a Roman numeral analysis for the following passages, making sure that you distinguish between essential and embellishing harmonies. Identify the circled embellishing tones on the music by using the usual abbreviations (see Chapter 7). The chord on the first beat of measure 7 in Example 10.9A is a I$^6_4$ chord, which functions here as a suspended dominant harmony.

Example 10.9A

A. "Sweet Bye and Bye" (American hymn tune)

G:

Example 10.9B

B. "Londonderry Air" (English folk song)

F#:

What is the additional cadence that is appended at the conclusion of Example 10.9C?

Example 10.9C

C. "Let All Mortal Flesh Keep Silent" (French carol)

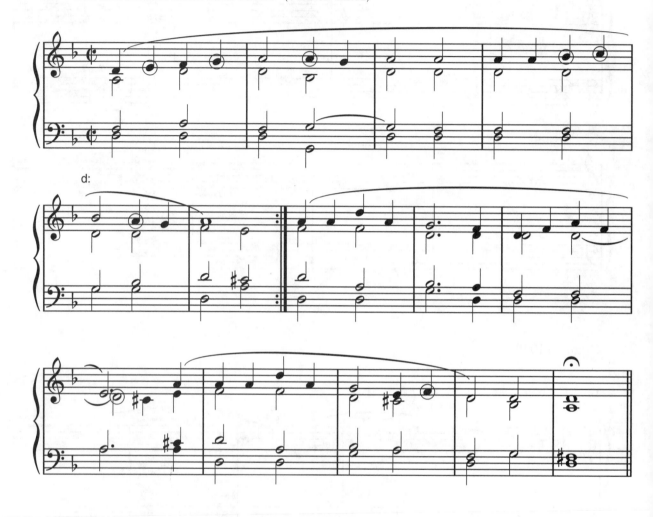

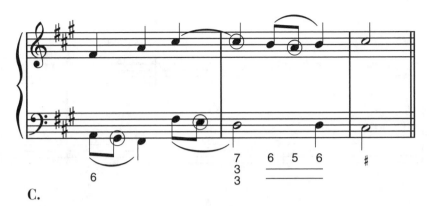

C.

D.

E.

A♭:

F.

g:

3 Choose two of the melodies below and harmonize them in four-voice texture, then add the appropriate Roman numerals to your completed setting. Try to insert a few embellishing I or IV chords. You may wish to review the harmonization guidelines for melodies in chorale style discussed in Chapter 11 of the text.

Example 11.3

A.

D:

B.

g♯

C.

E♭:

4 Using the two harmonic models below, elaborate these progressions into passages of actual music, similar to those that appear near the end of Chapter 11. Choose your own meter, tempo, dynamics, slurring, and rhythmic values but maintain the same approximate rate of chord change, about two per measure. If you are in doubt about the use of any embellishing tones, refer to the definitions and examples in Chapter 7.

Example 11.4

A.

E:

B.

g:

5 After analyzing the following three passages with Roman numerals, make a voice-leading reduction of each. For the first two exercises a two-part framework (soprano and bass) is sufficient, but in the last passage include all three voices in the reduction. Be sure that you distinguish between essential and embellishing harmonies, connecting the latter to the former with slurs. Since the embellishing tones are not circled in the last two examples, you must determine which tones are consonant and dissonant.

Example 11.5

A.

c:

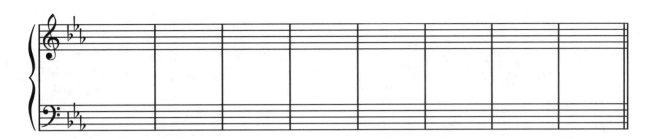

B.

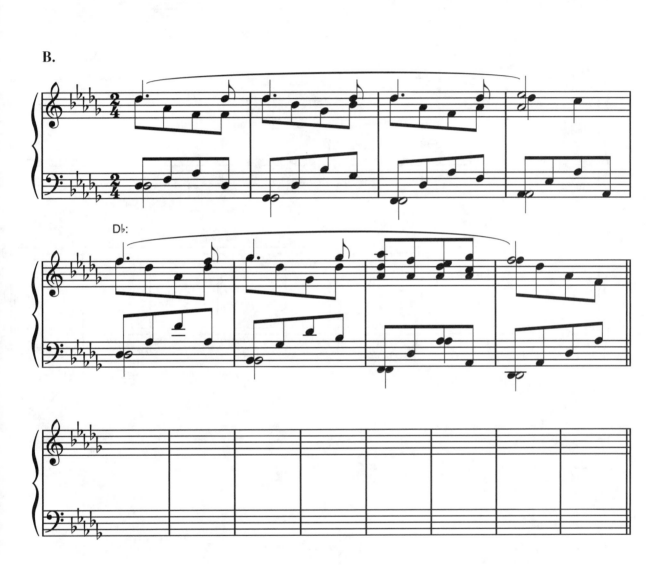

C.

b:

Example 12.3

BACH: TWO-PART INVENTION IN C MAJOR

4   This excerpt, given in simplified form, contains a principal melody in the upper flute part and an underlying motivic idea that assumes a secondary or accompanimental role in the texture. Identify this motive and circle all its appearances, noting any examples of melodic inversion or mirroring.

Example 12.4

BRAHMS: SYMPHONY NO. 1 IN C MINOR, IV

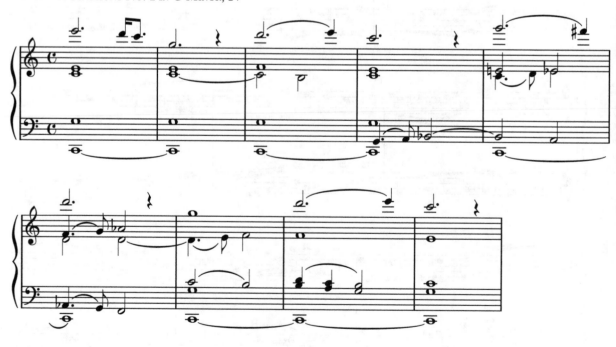

C H A P T E R   1 3

Linear Dominants:

V⁶, VII°⁶, AND INVERSIONS OF V⁷

1 Write the correct inversion of the indicated dominant family chord on the staff;
the first two are done for you.

Example 13.1

2 In each example a V^6, vii^{o6}, or an inverted V^7 is quoted in a given key. Using four-voice texture, resolve each chord correctly to either I or I^6. In the case of the seventh chords, make certain that the chordal 7th moves downward by step. In your Roman numeral analysis, remember that the linear dominant is placed in parentheses. Follow the model of the first example.

Example 13.2

a: (V⁶)   i   D: b♭:   g:

A: c: f: e:

F: B:

3 Each short progression below features an unstemmed embellishing dominant as its middle chord. In addition to the key and figured-bass symbols, the first soprano note is supplied for each example. Complete the progression in four-voice texture and supply a Roman numeral analysis. In the examples that use V⁷ chords, the type of preparation and resolution for the chordal 7th is indicated above the soprano. Follow the model of the first example.

Example 13.3

4 Realize the following figured-bass exercises, and supply a Roman numeral analysis, enclosing any embellishing dominants in parentheses.

Example 13.4A

A.

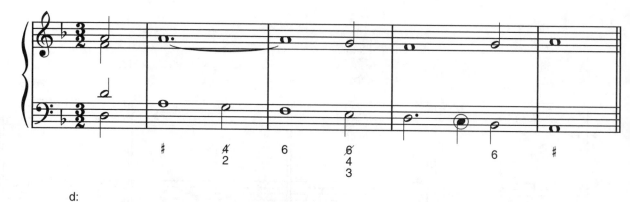

d:

Example 13.4B

B.

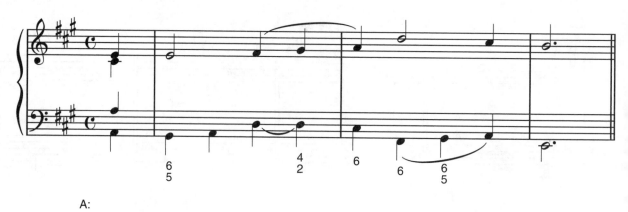

A:

Example 13.4C

C.

A♭:

Example 13.4D

D.

c#:

Since the bass in Example 13.4E is unfigured, you must deduce the implied harmonies from the outer voices.

Example 13.4E

E.

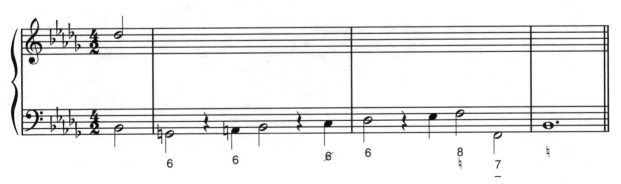

b:

Supply your own soprano line in Example 13.4F; the first note is given.

Example 13.4F

F.

bb:

5 In the following excerpts, find the examples of (1) a displaced 7th, (2) a prolonged dominant, (3) a delayed resolution, or (4) a resolution of the chordal 7th in a different voice. Write your answers on the lines provided below the staff.

Example 13.5

A. BEETHOVEN: PIANO SONATA IN E-FLAT MAJOR, OP. 81A ("LES ADIEUX"), I

B. MOZART: SYMPHONY NO. 41 IN C MAJOR ("JUPITER"), II

C. HAYDN: PIANO SONATA IN C MAJOR, HOB. XVI, NO. 21, II

D. Bach: Recitative from Cantata No. 80, *Ein' feste Burg ist unser Gott*

statt!　Lass　nicht dein Herz,　den Him-mel Got-tes auf　der　Er - den,

E. Chopin: Waltz in A-flat Major, Op. 69, No. 1

6　Harmonize two of the three melodies below in a four-voice setting. Be sure to use standard cadence formulas and work out an interesting bass line by employing various inversions or embellishing dominants. Don't forget the possibility of adding some embellishing tones. Then provide a Roman numeral analysis of your harmonization.

Example 13.6

A.

F:

B.

b:

C.

E:

7 The piano sonatas of Beethoven contain a number of themes that utilize only tonic and dominant harmonies. Three of these are quoted below. Make a voice-leading reduction of each, indicating the embellishing chords with unstemmed notes and the essential harmonies with stemmed notes. Use appropriate slurs to connect the chords and supply a Roman numeral analysis. Consider the following questions about these excerpts, although it is not necessary that you write them out as part of your assignment.

A. How is the D♭³ (the chordal 7th) approached in the bass voice in measure one? Do you think this passage might qualify as an example of an embedded voice-leading motion?

Example 13.7A

BEETHOVEN: PIANO SONATA IN C MINOR, OP. 13 ("PATHÉTIQUE"), II

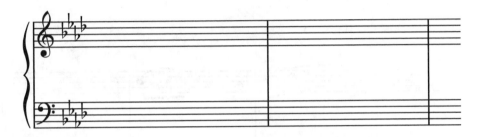

B. Which voice provides the greatest melodic interest? Does this opening section remind you of a particular kind of piece? To confirm your opinion, check Beethoven's title for this movement.

Example 13.7B

BEETHOVEN: PIANO SONATA IN A-FLAT MAJOR, OP. 26, III

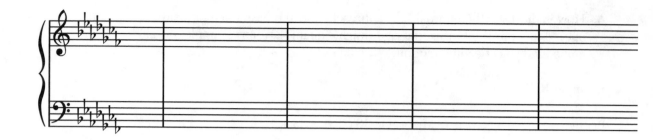

C. Before you complete your voice-leading graph, you must answer the following question: Does the V^4_3 in measure 3 embellish tonic harmony, or does the i chord in measure 3 embellish dominant harmony? Can you make a better case for one of these answers?

Example 13.7C

BEETHOVEN: PIANO SONATA IN D MAJOR, OP. 10, NO. 3, I

8 The following two excerpts contain instances of extended tonic prolongations using progressions of several different chords, such as I–(IV–vii°⁶)–I⁶. Supply a Roman numeral analysis of each excerpt, making certain that all embellishing chords or progressions are enclosed in parentheses.

A. Treat this passage as one long phrase.

Example 13.8A

"St. Theodulph" (hymn tune)

B. What is the function of measures 4–5 in this excerpt?

Example 13.8B

Brahms: Symphony No. 3 in F Major, II

9   Compose an original parallel period (4 + 4 measures) for piano using only the chords we have studied thus far. You may select your own texture, but continue to employ the partwriting procedures discussed up to this point. Maintain a relatively slow rate of harmonic change (one or two chords per measure), and try to include some embellishing dominants or progressions. You may use the motive listed below or choose your own melodic ideas.

Example 13.9

3 The following two melody harmonizations contain various partwriting problems or inappropriate chord choices. Circle the ones you find and describe them briefly, citing measure numbers, in the space provided. What is peculiar about the ii° in the first measure of the second setting?_____

_____

Example 14.3

A.

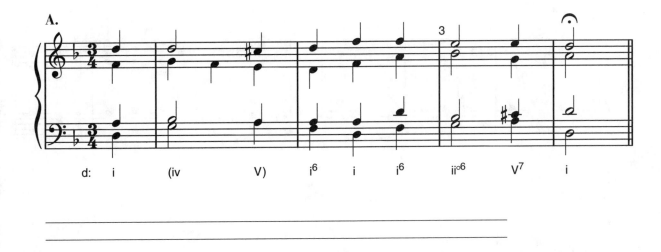

_____
_____
_____

B.

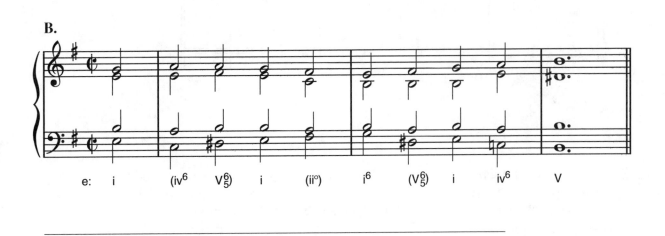

_____
_____
_____

4 Supply Roman numeral analyses for the passages below, placing parentheses around any embellishing pre-dominant chords. For each supertonic seventh chord, indicate whether the chordal 7th is treated as a suspension (S), passing tone (P), or incomplete neighbor (IN). There is an instance of parallel 5ths hidden in one of the below examples; can you find it?

Example 14.4

A.

bb:

B.

A:

C.

B:

5 In the following short progressions, the key, Roman numerals, inversions, and soprano lines are given. Complete each example in four-voice texture, paying particular attention to the preparation and resolution of any supertonic seventh chords.

Example 14.5

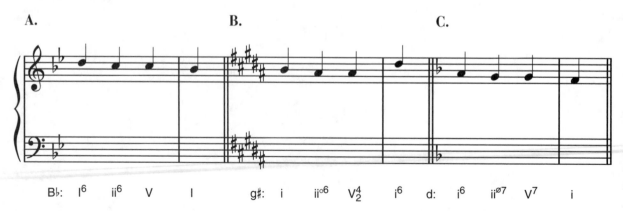

A.   B.   C.

Bb: I⁶   ii⁶   V   I   g#: i   ii°⁶   V⁴₂   i⁶   d: i⁶   ii⌀⁷   V⁷   i

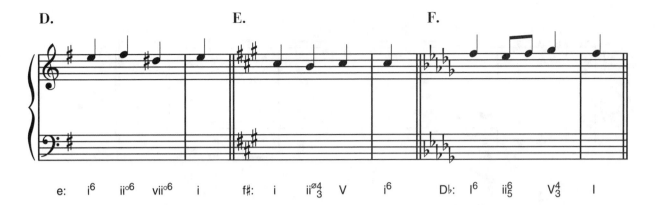

e: i⁶   ii°⁶   vii°⁶   i   f♯: i   ii°⁴₃   V   i⁶   D♭: I⁶   ii⁶₅   V⁴₃   I

6 Fill in the inner voices in the following figured-bass exercises and provide a Roman numeral analysis. Example 5H is unfigured; you must deduce the harmonies from the outer voices.

Example 14.6

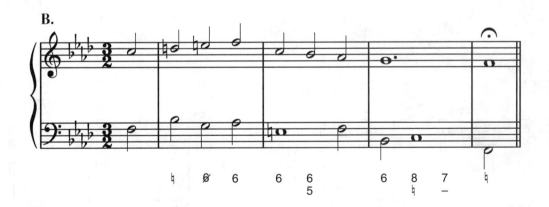

H.

7 Make a four-voice setting of two of the following three melodies, employing appropriate supertonic triads or seventh chords. Give a Roman numeral analysis of your settings. Try to compose a line of running eighth notes in the bass for Example 14.7B; what type of cadence will you use in E major? Example 14.7C requires a slower harmonic rhythm, about one chord per measure.

Example 14.7

A. "O HAUPT VOLL BLUT UND WUNDEN"

Eb:

B. "WIE SCHÖN LEUCHTET DER MORGENSTERN"

C.

8 Harmonize the melodic period below in a four-voice texture, using a different inversion of the supertonic seventh on each note marked with an arrow. Strive for an interesting bass line and provide a Roman numeral analysis.

Example 14.8

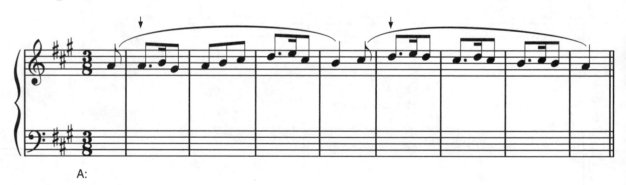

A:

9 Provide a Roman numeral analysis for the following excerpts.

A. Make a voice-leading graph of this passage in the blank staves. What soprano note is supported by the bass G^2 in the third measure? _____

Example 14.9A

VIVALDI: CONCERTO FOR FLUTE IN D MAJOR, II

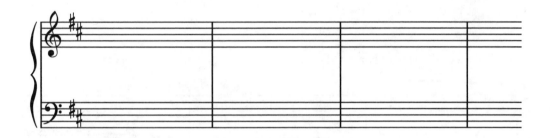

B. Why must the supertonic seventh be incomplete? _____

Example 14.9B

HANDEL: "LASCIA CH'IO PIANGA" FROM *RINALDO*, ACT II

C. What is the function of the chords on the second quarter notes of measures 5–8? _____

Example 14.9C

BEETHOVEN: SYMPHONY NO. 2 IN D MAJOR, III

D. Does this passage represent a cadential or embellishing progression? _____

Example 14.9D

BACH: SONATA FOR FLUTE AND CLAVIER IN E-FLAT MAJOR, II

E. Make a voice-leading diagram in the provided staves. In which measure
does the supertonic seventh chord appear in this famous horn solo? _____
What is its inversion? _____

Example 14.9E

TCHAIKOVSKY: SYMPHONY NO. 5 IN E MINOR, II

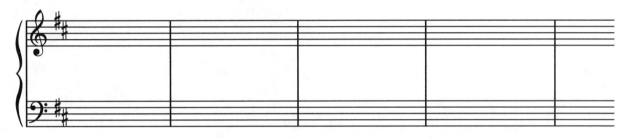

F. To what chord does the supertonic seventh resolve? _____
What is unusual about the resolution of its chordal 7th? _____
_____

Example 14.9F

MOZART: PIANO SONATA IN F MAJOR, K.280, II

C H A P T E R   1 5

Melodic Figuration and Dissonance II:

SUSPENSIONS AND OTHER EMBELLISHING TONES

1   **A.** To each three-note suspension figure below, add another consonant voice either below or above to complete the indicated two-part suspension. Make sure your rhythmic setting is correct.

Example 15.1A

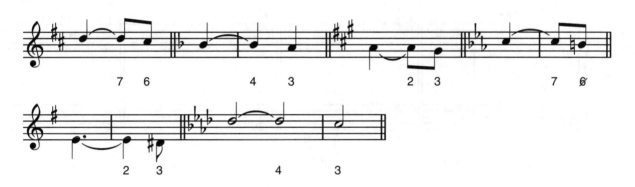

B. To each consonant voice below, add another voice either above or below that will produce the indicated dissonant suspension figure.

Example 15.1B

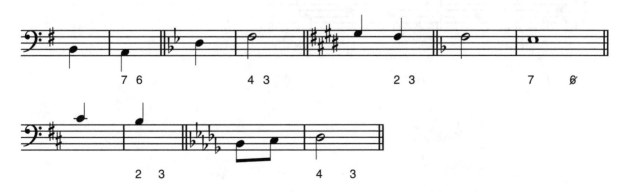

2 Fill in the inner voices according to the figured bass, preparing and resolving the indicated suspension correctly (usually ♩♫). Then provide Roman numerals. Be careful of accidentals in minor keys.

Example 15.2

3 Recopy the passage in 15.3A and add the appropriate suspensions in the upper or lower voice for those chords marked with an arrow.

Example 15.3A

A.

In Examples 15.3B and C only the consonant framework is given. Supply appropriate suspensions on those notes marked with arrows in either the top or bottom voice. Indicate each suspension with the proper figured-bass symbols. Try to use some suspensions involving change of bass or upper part.

Examples 15.3B and C

B.

C.

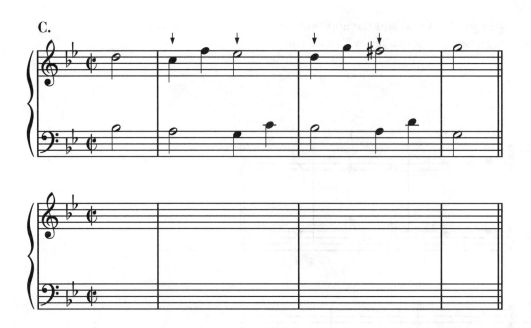

4 Given the following bass lines, figured-bass symbols, and rhythmic patterns above some of the staves, write out the indicated suspensions in four-voice texture. Example 15.4A is started for you. Guard against doubling the note of resolution in 7-6, 4-3, and 2-3 suspensions. Then provide a Roman numeral analysis. You will notice that the figured bass becomes rather complicated in some of these examples. Actually, this works to your advantage; just be careful to write what the figures indicate.

Example 15.4

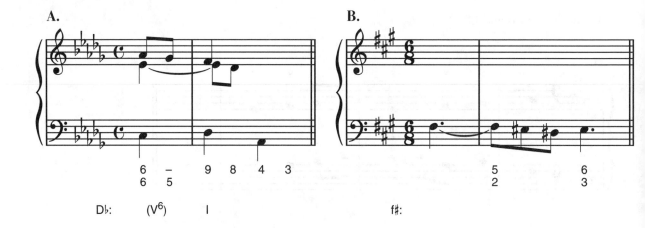

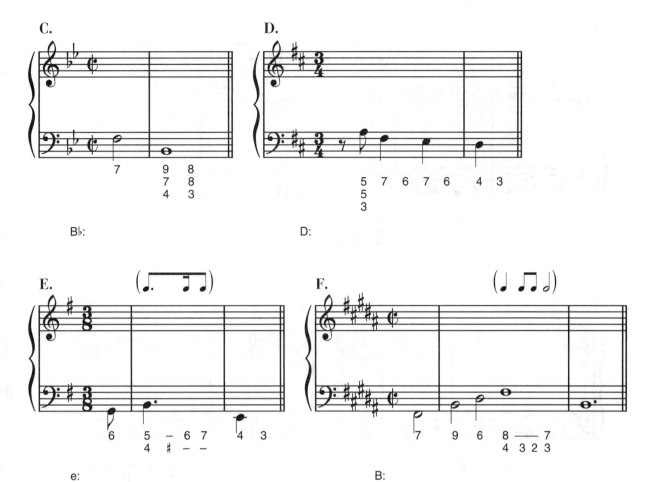

5   Realize the following figured-bass examples in four-voice texture and provide a
    Roman numeral analysis. In Example 15.5B the figures at the beginning of the
    second full measure indicate that you should double the 5th above the bass;
    possible rhythmic patterns are suggested above the staff. Be especially careful
    about what notes you double in Example 15.5C to avoid parallel perfect
    intervals. Finally, although Example 15.5E is unfigured, more than one
    suspension is suggested by the outer voices.

Example 15.5

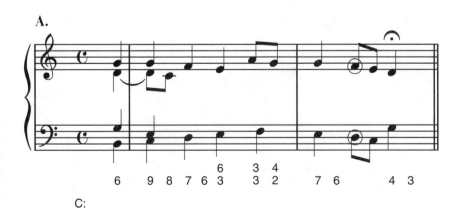

B.

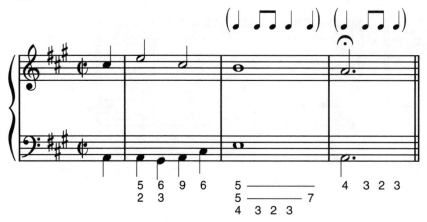

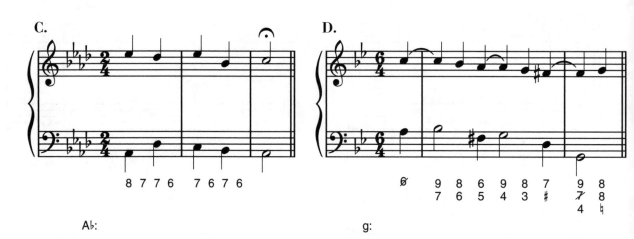

A:

C.

A♭:

D.

g:

E.

f:

6 Harmonize the following two melodic lines in a four-voice setting, using our current vocabulary of harmonies. Add a variety of appropriate suspensions to your settings. The chords change only once a measure in the first tune; they move at a faster rate in the chorale melody.

Example 15.6

A.

E:

B. "Jesu, deine tiefen Wunden"

B♭:

7 Identify the various suspensions in the following excerpts by notating the correct figured-bass symbols below the staff: 4-3, 7-6, etc. It is not necessary to analyze the harmonies.

A. What do you notice about the suspension resolutions in this passage?

Example 15.7A

Mozart: Rondo in F Major, K.494

B. In what two ways can the suspension in the last measure of this excerpt be analyzed?

Example 15.7B

THOMAS ARNE: THREE-VOICE CANON

C. On the staff provided, reduce this compound melody to its constituent parts in order to reveal the suspensions within its implied two voices.

Example 15.7C

COUPERIN: "LA MILORDINE" FROM *PREMIÈRE ORDRE*

8 The Prelude in B Minor from Volume 1 of Bach's *Well-Tempered Clavier* is a study in suspension technique. Make a three-voice reduction of its first four measures on the staves provided below, indicating the types of suspensions with figured-bass symbols. Watch for the half notes that occur on beats 2 and 4, as they may produce suspension dissonances on the next beat. Also, watch for changes of bass; there are no less than five in these few measures.

Example 15.8

BACH: PRELUDE IN B MINOR FROM *THE WELL-TEMPERED CLAVIER*, BOOK I

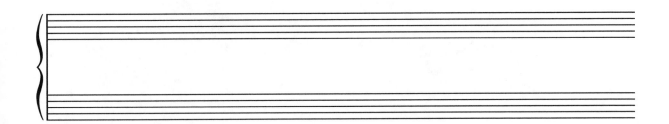

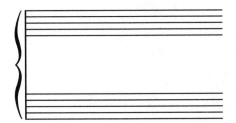

C. This opening passage from this unusual Czech oratorio prominently features pre-dominant harmonies. What is the function of the chords on the third beat of measures 1 and 2 during this prolongation? _____

_____

Example 16.4C

Krsto Zyžik: *Dieta Wormsová*

D. In which section of this Mendelssohn piece would the following passage most likely occur? _____

Example 16.4D

Mendelssohn: *Songs without Words*, Op. 38, No. 1

5 Realize the following figured-bass examples. Label each $^6_4$ chord using the abbreviations listed in Question 3. Supply a Roman numeral analysis, taking care to distinguish between essential and embellishing harmonies. Examples 16.5B and E are unfigured; in Example 16.5F you must supply your own soprano line.

Example 16.5

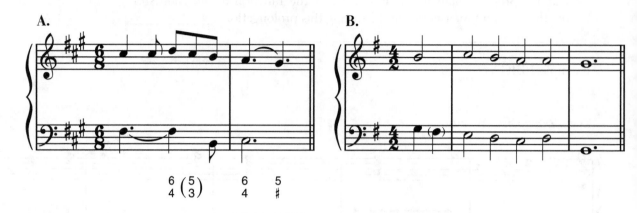

A.

B.

$$
\begin{array}{ccccc}
6 & \left(\begin{array}{c}5\\3\end{array}\right) & & 6 & 5 \\
4 & & & 4 & \sharp
\end{array}
$$

C.

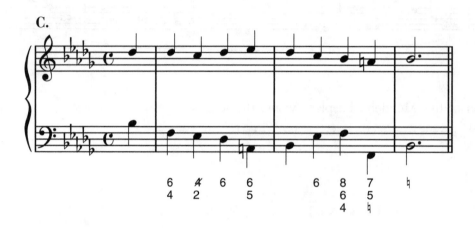

$$
\begin{array}{cccccccc}
6 & \not4 & 6 & 6 & & 6 & 8 & 7 & \natural \\
4 & 2 & & 5 & & & 6 & 5 & \\
& & & & & & 4 & \natural &
\end{array}
$$

D.

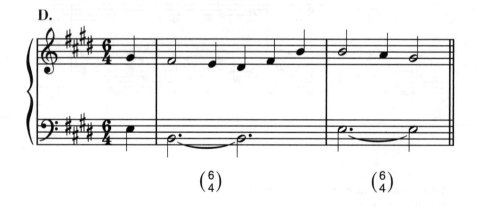

$$
\left(\begin{array}{c}6\\4\end{array}\right) \qquad\qquad \left(\begin{array}{c}6\\4\end{array}\right)
$$

E.

f:

F.

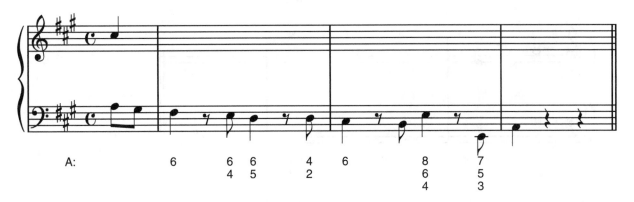

A: 6   6 6   4   6   8   7
        4 5   2   6   5
                     4   3

6 Complete the following passages, using the Roman numerals as your guide. After writing in the bass part, complete an appropriate soprano line; some soprano notes are supplied. Then fill in the alto and tenor voices and indicate below each example the type of $^6_4$ it employs, using the abbreviations listed in Question 3.

Example 16.6

A.   B.

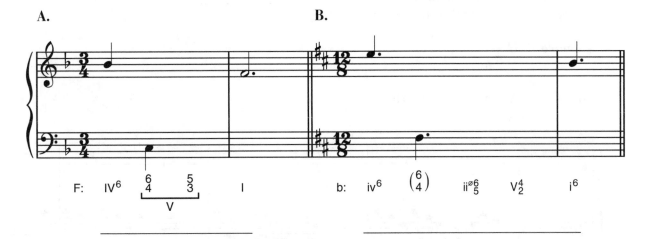

F: IV^6 $^6_4$ $^5_3$ I   b: iv^6 $\left(^6_4\right)$ ii$^{ø6}_5$ V$^4_2$ i^6
       ⌞__V__⌟

_____   _____

C.   D.

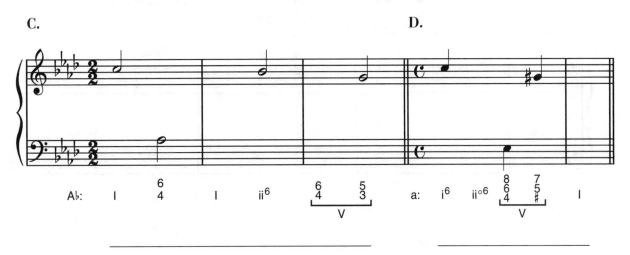

A♭: I $^6_4$ I ii^6 $^6_4$ $^5_3$ a: i^6 ii^{o6} $^8_6{}_4$ $^7_5{}_{\sharp}$ I
                ⌞__V__⌟   ⌞__V__⌟

_____   _____

E.

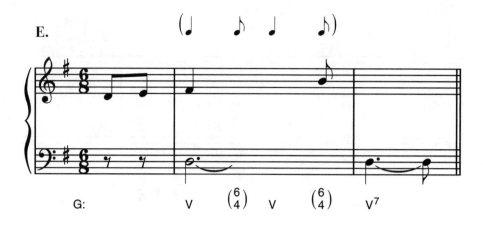

G: V $\binom{6}{4}$ V $\binom{6}{4}$ V⁷

---

7 Make voice-leading reductions for the following two excerpts, then provide a Roman numeral analysis of each. Be sure to identify the various types of $^6_4$ chords employed in each.

A. What voice-leading device occurs between the soprano and upper voice of the accompaniment in measures 1–2? _____
Be sure to indicate this correctly on your graph.

Example 16.7A

HAYDN: PIANO SONATA IN C MAJOR, HOB. XVI, No. 35, I

(vi)

B. Is the same device used in the first two measures of this passage? _____
Note the F^5 in the soprano on the second half of the first beat in measure 3.
In which voice part do you think that note resolves? _____

Example 16.7B

MOZART: PIANO SONATA IN C MAJOR K.330, III

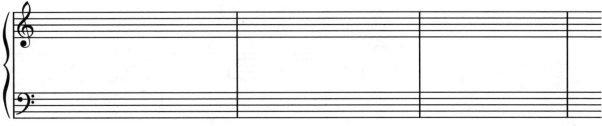

8 Harmonize this melodic period in a four-voice setting. Each soprano note marked with an arrow should be supported with an appropriate $^6_4$ chord. Provide a Roman numeral analysis of your harmonization.

Example 16.8

G♭:

9 Circle any instances of linear chords produced by passing motion, neighboring motion, etc., in the following passage. Then make a harmonic reduction that indicates the essential chords with stemmed notes and embellishing tones with unstemmed notes; follow the model of the opening measure.

Example 16.9

C.

A: 6   5   7   6   6   6   5   7   4   3

D.

c: 6   6   6   ♮

7 Provide Roman numeral analyses for the following excerpts.

A. The relation between the bass dotted-half notes and the upper eighth-note motion is acceptable. What do you think about the voice leading between the bass and the tenor quarter notes? _____

_____

Example 17.7A

ALESSANDRO SCARLATTI: *FOLIA*

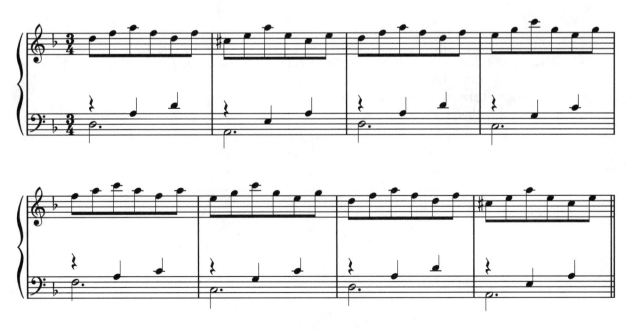

B. Make a voice-leading reduction of this passage; the upper staff may contain two linear strands. Add the usual Roman numerals.

Example 17.7B

WAGNER: "FORGING SONG" FROM *SIEGFRIED*, ACT I

C. Tchaikovsky's *Romeo and Juliet* Overture-Fantasy opens with a musical portrayal of Friar Lawrence, the priest in Shakespeare's drama. What appropriate harmonic or tonal procedure has the composer used to heighten this characterization? _____

Can you find an example of parallel octaves and fifths in this passage? If so, where? _____

_____

Name _____

Example 17.7C

Tchaikovsky: *Romeo and Juliet*, Overture-Fantasy

Example 19.3

A.

d:

B.

b:

C.

e:

D.

b♭:

E.

c♯:

F.

A♭:

4 Realize the following figured-bass exercises and provide a Roman numeral analysis for each passage. Indicate how each chordal seventh is prepared and resolved by using an appropriate abbreviation. In Example 19.4D, which is unfigured, try to use at least two vii°⁷s. In Example 19.4E you must supply your own soprano.

Example 19.4

A.

B.

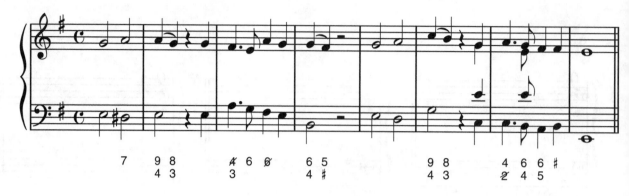

C.

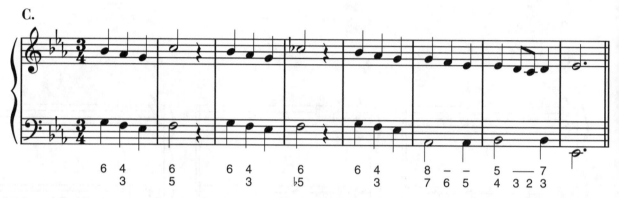

D.

E.

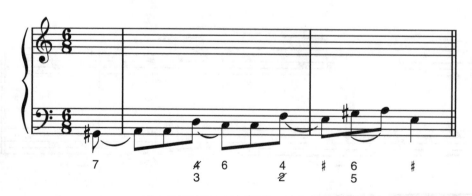

5 Harmonize the two melodies below, using a vii°⁷ or one of its inversions to support the soprano notes marked with an arrow. In the second example, the melody appears in the bass voice.

Example 19.5

A.

B.

6 Analyze the following excerpts with Roman numerals and circle any non-harmonic tones; be sure to distinguish between essential and embellishing harmonies.

A. This passage is especially rich in leading-tone seventh chords. What is the underlying harmony in the first eight measures? _____

Example 19.6A

GLUCK: "THROUGH THIS GROVE" FROM *ORFEO ED EURIDICE*, ACT I

vii°7/V

B. Make a reduction of this phrase. What voice-leading device do you notice in measures 2–3? _____ How does Brahms emphasize his leading-tone sevenths? _____ _____ How do you think the last chord in measure 4 functions? _____

Example 19.6B

BRAHMS: BALLADE IN B MAJOR, OP. 10, NO. 4

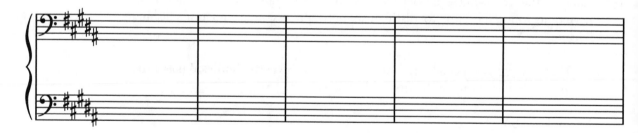

C. The key signature of this quotation is misleading, since the tonal center is actually E-flat minor. What type of embellishing tone occurs in the first three measures? _____ Locate a diminished seventh chord that is not built on the leading tone. _____

Example 19.6C

FRANCK: PRELUDE, CHORALE, AND FUGUE FOR PIANO

D. This very interesting passage contains numerous accented embellishing tones and a double meter signature. Provide a voice-leading reduction and Roman numeral analysis.

Your first problem is to find the key center; don't rely on the key signature but look near the end of the excerpt. What chord is prolonged through the first two beats of measure 4? _____ What do you notice about the soprano line in measures 5–7? _____ _____ The final cadence features a typical Wagnerian deceptive cadence.

Example 19.6D

WAGNER: *DIE WALKÜRE,* ACT II, SCENE 3

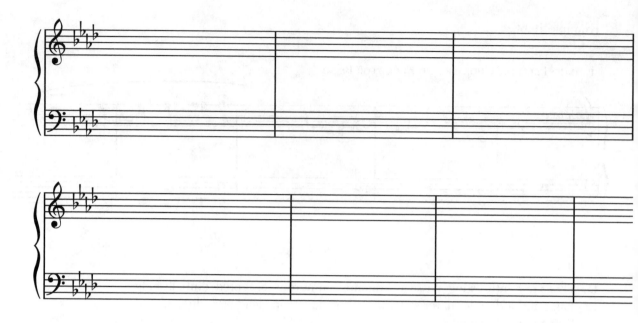

7 In the short progressions below, which incorporate subdominant and tonic seventh chords, the key, Roman numerals, inversions, and soprano lines have been provided for you. Fill in the remaining voices in four-part texture, observing the proper preparation and resolution of any seventh chords. Be wary of possible parallel fifths in the first two examples.

Example 19.7

8 Fill in the inner voices of the following figured-bass exercises and provide a
Roman numeral analysis.

Example 19.8

A.

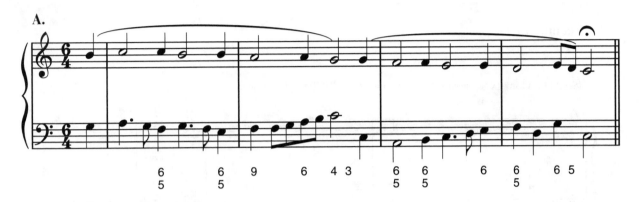

B.

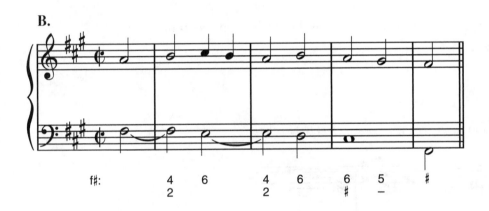

C.

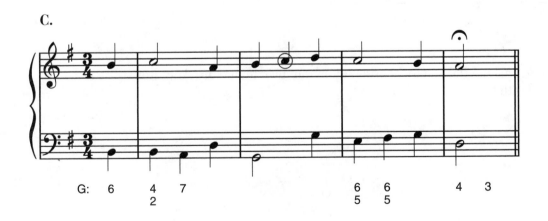

9 Provide a Roman numeral analysis of the following short excerpts.

A. How does Corelli avoid the potential parallel fifths between measures 4 and 5? _____

_____

Example 19.9A

CORELLI: CORRENTE FROM CONCERTO GROSSO No. 10 IN C MAJOR

B. Schumann's three-star designation for this lovely little piece remains a mystery.

Example 19.9B

SCHUMANN: "★★★" FROM *ALBUM FOR THE YOUNG*, OP. 68, No. 30

C. In your analysis, take into consideration the two temporary key areas marked with brackets.

Example 19.9C

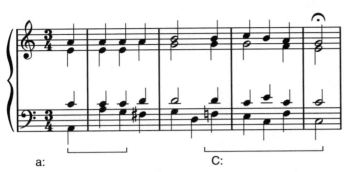

"Puer natus in Bethlehem" (Bach chorale harmonization)

10 Compose an original parallel period that employs the diatonic triads and seventh chords we have studied thus far. You may write either a three- or four-voice setting and use some occasional octave doublings. Strive for good melodic lines in the outer parts, and add a few embellishing tones when appropriate. The key, meter, and tempo are up to you. Then analyze your results with Roman numerals; you might even wish to make a voice-leading reduction.

Example 19.10

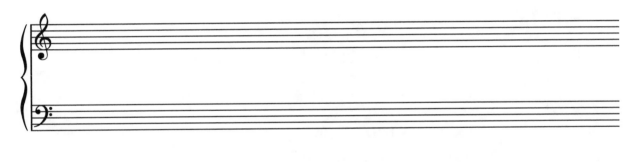

B.

e: 6   #

C.

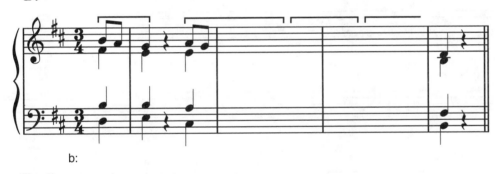

D:

D.

b:

E.

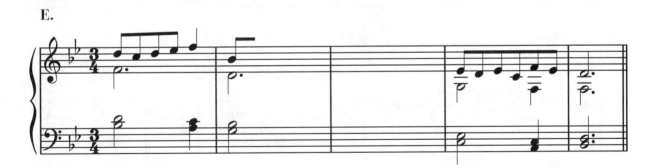

3 On the staves below each passage, elaborate the following three-voice sequence models. Your figuration should remain the same until the sequential motion ends. Choose your own meter and motivic ideas, being careful that you do not create parallels. Identify each type of sequence with figured-bass symbols. One possible elaboration is given below Example 20.3A.

Example 20.3

A. (MODEL)

B.

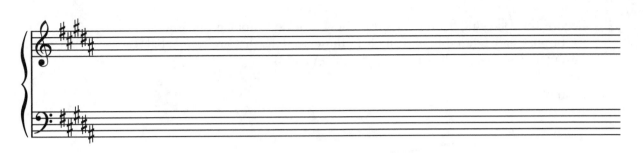

C.

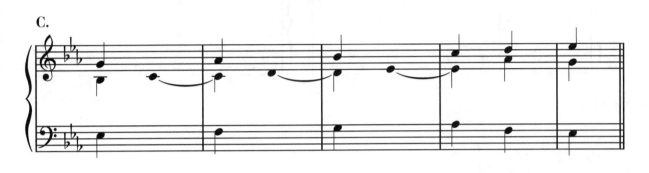

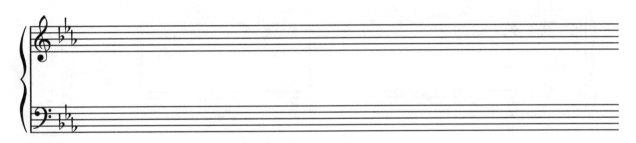

D.

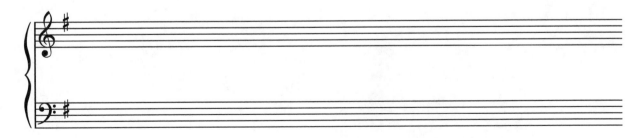

[CH. 20] HARMONIC SEQUENCES I **169**

4 Realize the following figured-bass exercises. Provide a Roman numeral analysis, but use only figured-bass symbols in those sections that are sequential. Be careful of potential parallels in Examples 20.4A and B.

Example 20.4

A.

B.

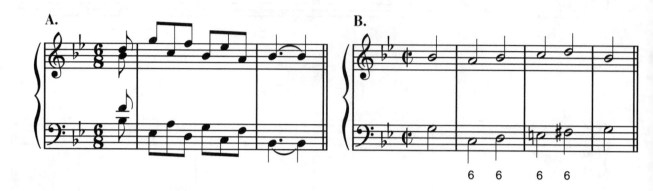

C.

D.

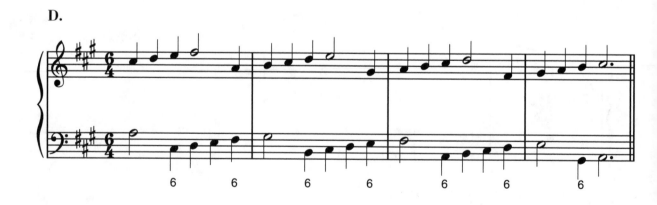

E.

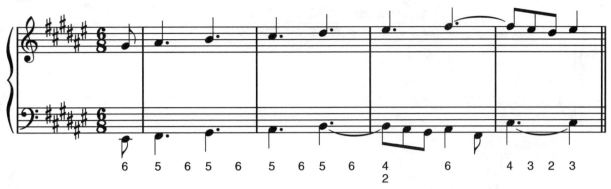

6 5 6 5 6   5 6 5 6   4   6   4 3 2 3
                              2

F.

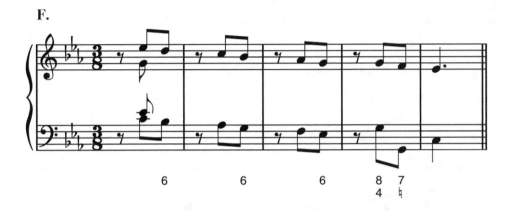

6   6   6   8 7
                           4 ♮

5 Harmonize the three melodies below, employing sequences when appropriate.
Try to incorporate some chordal inversions in your bass line.

Example 20.5

A. "BINGO" (FOLK SONG)

F:

B.

a:

C.

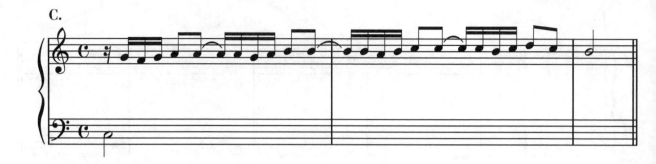

6 The following excerpts exhibit various types of diatonic sequences. Make voice-leading reductions of Examples 20.6B, D, and E. Label the essential or framing harmonies with Roman numerals and the sequential motion with figured-bass symbols.

A. What is the function of the chords on the second beat of the first six measures? _____

Example 20.6A

BEETHOVEN: SYMPHONY NO. 5 IN C MINOR, I

B. What type of embellishing tone does Handel use to elaborate this sequence? _____

Example 20.6B

HANDEL: "SURELY HE HAS BORNE OUR GRIEF" FROM *MESSIAH*

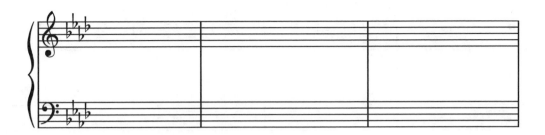

C. What type of embellishing dissonance momentarily disguises the soprano motion in measures 2–4? _____

Example 20.6C

Gluck: *Alceste*, Act III

Leb'   ein - ge - denk ____ der Zärt-lich - keit ____   ei - ner   Gat - tin

D. Note the pun in the title. How is the $\frac{5}{4}$ meter grouped? _____

Example 20.6D

Paul Desmond: "Take Five"

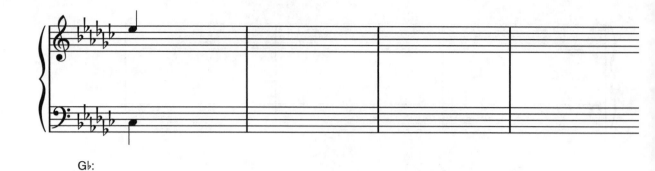

G♭:

E. This passage employs a two-voice texture. In order to show the alternating root-position and first-inversion chords, it is necessary to imply a third voice that fills out the harmony; see the opening of the analysis.

Example 20.6E

Scarlatti: Sonata in F Major, K. 518

F.

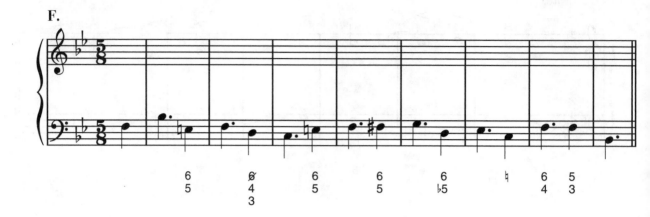

5 Harmonize the following two melodies, using an appropriate secondary dominant at each arrow. Supply a Roman numeral analysis of your settings. Your finished versions should include a tonicization of the five basic diatonic triads in the given mode other than the tonic.

Example 21.5

6 The following excerpts contain various uses of secondary dominant triads and seventh chords. Provide a Roman numeral analysis for each example, and provide a voice-leading reduction for Examples 21.6A and E.

C H A P T E R   2 2

Tonicization and Modulation II:

MODULATION TO V AND III

1 **A.** For the following triads, provide proper Roman numerals and inversion signs to indicate chord function in the keys of F major and G minor. Assuming each chord is a pivot chord in a modulation from F major to V and from G minor to III, write the function each chord has in the new key. The first chord in each example is completed for you.

Example 22.1A

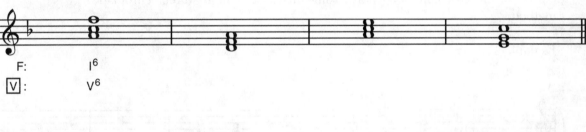

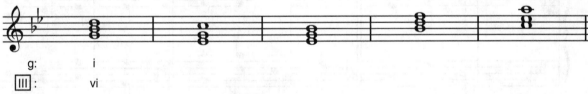

B. For the following triads, indicate how they function in the original key, then directly below how they function as pivot chords in the key areas of V, modulating from a major key, or in III, modulating from a minor key. Follow the models provided.

Example 22.1B

D: V

[V]:   I

g: iv

[III]:   ii

2   The following four-chord progressions feature a modulation from a tonic major to the dominant or from a minor key to the relative major. Provide a Roman numeral analysis, using Example A as your model. Most of these exercises employ a pivot or common chord; some may use a more direct chromatic method.

Example 22.2

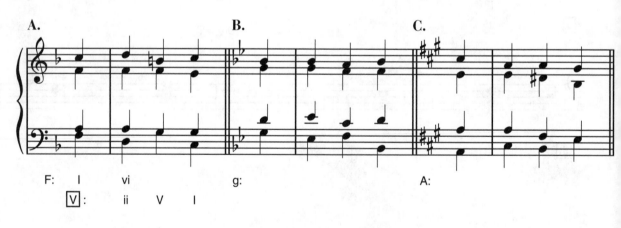

F: I   vi   g: A:

[V]: ii   V   I

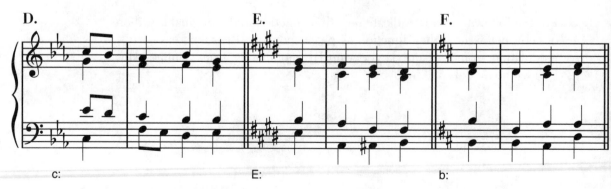

c: E: b:

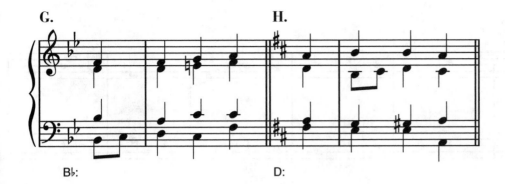

B♭:   D:

3 The following figured-bass exercises consist of two phrases each. After the first phrase modulates to either $\boxed{V}$ or $\boxed{III}$, the second phrase returns to the original key. Fill in the alto and tenor voices, and supply a Roman numeral analysis. If you need a pivot chord to modulate, be sure to indicate it correctly in your analysis. Example 22.3C is mostly unfigured.

Example 22.3

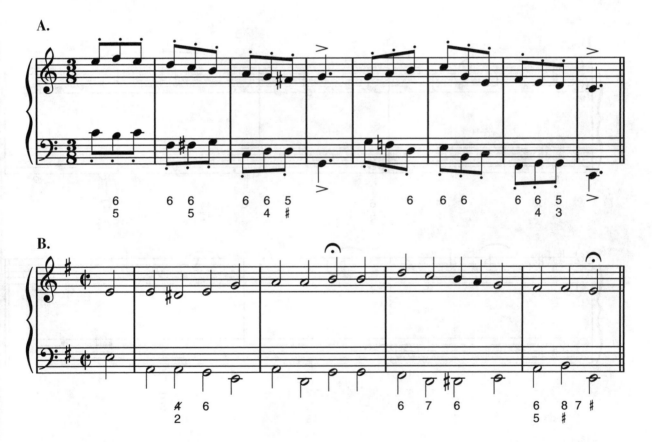

4 The following phrases modulate to the dominant $\boxed{V}$ or the relative major $\boxed{III}$. The original key, pivot chord, and soprano line are supplied for you. Compose an appropriate chord progression in four-voice texture to complete each exercise, making sure that you arrive at a convincing cadence in the new key. Then provide a Roman numeral analysis. What kind of modulation occurs in Example 22.4E? _____

Example 22.4

A.

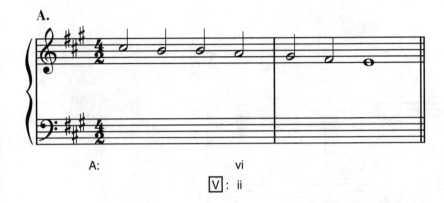

A: vi
$\boxed{V}$: ii

B.

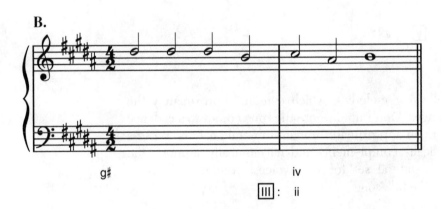

g#   iv
$\boxed{III}$: ii

C.

F: I
$\boxed{V}$: IV

D.

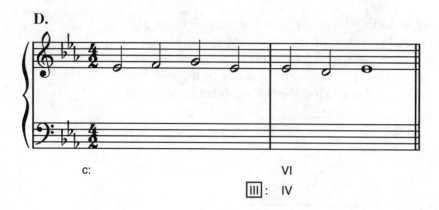

c: VI

$\boxed{\text{III}}$: IV

E.

E: ii⁶

$\boxed{\text{V}}$: V^6_5

5   Harmonize one of the following melodies, which contain approximately the same number of chord changes. Determine where the tune comes to a cadence in a new key, then sketch in an approximate Roman numeral analysis. Write a good bass line that melodically complements and harmonically supports the tune. The chorale tune should be set for four voices; you may choose a different type of texture for the folk song.

Example 22.5

A. "THE VICAR OF BRAY"

B. "Sei gegrüsset, Jesu gütig"

g:

6 Excerpts from two minuets are cited below; both have modulations to and from the dominant or relative major key.

A. Make a voice-leading analysis of this Beethoven trio in the empty staves and provide a Roman numeral analysis below. Since this passage is in two-voice texture, you will have to deduce the implied harmonies as in unfigured-bass exercises; in some measures, you may wish to employ a kind of compound melody reduction. Use brackets above the staff to mark the extent of each phrase. You may find several secondary dominants in the first section. The voice leading of the last phrase is a bit tricky. Remember that since the harmonies change here only once per measure, one soprano note per measure will suffice. Choose the one that will produce the smoothest motion.

What happens tonally in measures 9–12? _____

_____

What rhythmic device does the slurring suggest in these four measures?

_____

Example 22.6A

Beethoven: Minuet in G, WoO 11, No. 2, Trio

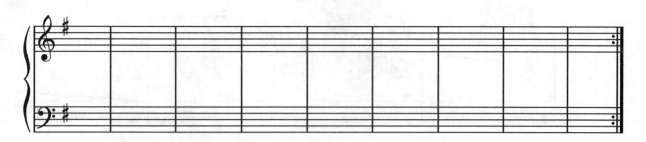

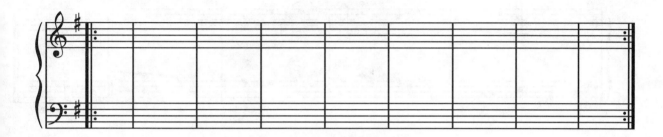

B. Provide a Roman numeral analysis of this piece. Why do you think the harmony in measure 12 is prolonged through measure 14? _____

_____

Example 22.6B

BACH(?): MINUET IN D MINOR FROM *ANNA MAGDALENA BACH'S NOTEBOOK*

7   Compose an original two-phrase period that modulates from a minor key to
[III] then returns to the original tonic. Strive for an interesting rhythmic setting.
You might use the harmonic scheme of one of the preceding exercises as your
model.

Example 22.7

C H A P T E R   2 3

Harmonic Sequences II:

SEQUENCES OF SEVENTH CHORDS AND OTHER SEQUENCES

1 Complete the following diatonic sequences employing seventh chords. Indicate the figured bass in the interior of the phrases.

Example 23.1

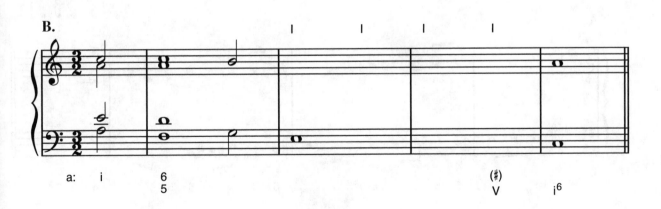

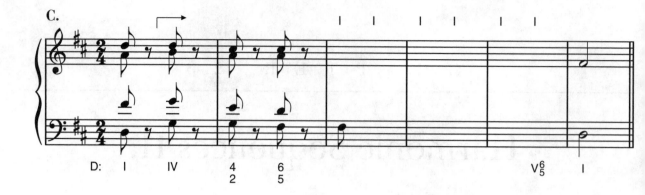

C.

D: I   IV   4/2   6/5   V6/5   I

D.

e: i   7   4/3   V7   i

2 Fill in the inner voices in the following figured-bass exercises. Mark off the units in the sequence of each example with a bracket and provide framing Roman numerals for the entire pattern.

Example 23.2

A.

f#:   6   5   6 ♮5   6   5   6   5   6   4   3   2   3

B.

g: 8 7   8 7   8 7 5 4 #
    5 6 5   5 6 5   5 6 5 # 2 8

C.

G: 6   6   6   6   6   4
        #4   5   #4   5   2
        2   2

    6   6   6
        4   5

3   Complete the following sequences and add the appropriate figured-bass symbols. Then indicate the underlying root movement of each bracketed pattern, such as ascending 3rd, descending 2nd, etc.

Example 23.3

A.

Ab: I

V

B.

A: I

C. _____

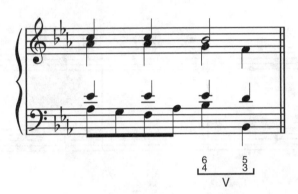

4 Harmonize the following melody, using a complete cycle of diatonic seventh chords in descending 5ths. Circle any instances of dissonant embellishing tones in the melodic line. In your setting you may, if you wish, use some texture other than a strict four-voice style.

Example 23.4

5 Bracket the sequence units in the first three excerpts below, then analyze them, using framing Roman numerals and the appropriate figured-bass symbols.

A. In his overture to *Don Giovanni,* Mozart provides us with an excellent motivic elaboration of a sequence, in this instance employing imitation between the upper voices. Make a voice-leading graph of this passage; the first chord has already been provided. Indicate the chord quality of each seventh chord.

Example 23.5A

MOZART: OVERTURE TO *DON GIOVANNI*

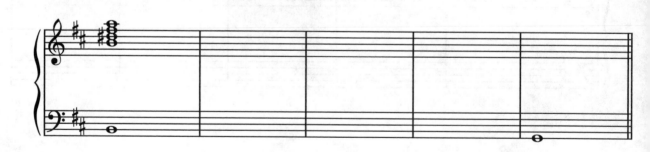

B. What meter is suggested by the sequence units within your brackets?

Example 23.5B

Bach: Three-part Invention in E Major

C. In the sequential portion of this excerpt, are all the harmonies diatonic
seventh chords? _____

    If not, which ones are different? _____

Example 23.5C

Wagner: Overture to *Die Meistersinger* (simplified)

D. An excerpt from a well-known operatic aria is given below. Considering the failing state of Mimì's health, the basic direction of the melody seems appropriate. Which voice part in the accompaniment doubles the vocal line at the octave? _____ Although this passage is not strictly sequential, it does contain some brief sequential portions. Analyze the entire passage with Roman numerals, then bracket that section that suggests a progression by descending 5ths.

Example 23.5D

PUCCINI: "SONO ANDATI?" FROM *LA BOHÈME*, ACT IV

so - la, ma gran-de co-me il ma - re, ____

. . . Fingevo di dormire
perchè volli con te sola restare.
Ho tante cose che ti voglio dire
o una sola, ma grande come il mare, . . .

. . . I pretended to sleep
because I wanted to remain alone with you.
I have so many things I want to say to you
or just one, but as large as the sea, . . .

C H A P T E R   2 4

Simple Forms

In addition to the pieces reproduced here and in the later Workbook chapter on form (Chapter 31), some other movements, largely selected from works of the Classical period, are recommended for analysis projects. Many of these pieces may be found in published anthologies of music.

ONE-PART FORM

This little Prelude in F Major appeared in Bach's *Clavierbüchlein*, a collection of short pieces he wrote for the keyboard instruction of his son Wilhelm Friedemann. The positioning of various harmonic sequences influences to a large degree the work's overall tonal structure, which is firmly rooted in the tonic key.

 Example 24.1

BACH: PRELUDE IN F MAJOR FROM *CLAVIERBÜCHLEIN*

Other pieces in one-part form include Bach's Prelude in C Minor for Lute, BWV 999, and Chopin's Prelude in B Minor, Op. 28, No. 6.

BINARY OR TWO-REPRISE FORM

Simple Two-Part Form (AB)

Some folk songs consist of two well-defined sections: verse (A) and refrain or chorus (B). For example, see "My Bonnie Lies over the Ocean" and "My Old Kentucky Home." Many chorale tunes, such as "Christ lag in Todesbanden" and "O Haupt voll Blut und Wunden," employ *bar form* (AAB).

Baroque Two-Reprise Form

Short examples of two-reprise form in the Baroque period may be found in Exercise 22.6B of this Workbook and Example 24.2 of the text. The dance movements in Baroque suites or partitas are cast in this design. The shorter movements, sarabandes or minuets, are usually less tonally complex. Also consult the brief minuets in Bach's *Notebook for Anna Magdelena Bach*.

Bach: Brandenburg Concerto No. 1 in F Major, IV. This movement contains four such sections. Which one employs a *rounded* binary form?

Handel: *Water Music* or *Royal Fireworks Music*. Many of the interior dance movements employ two-reprise form.

Scarlatti: Almost any of his so-called Sonatas—for instance, the Sonata in D Minor, L. 413/K.9.

Classical Two-Reprise Form

The minuet and trio sections of Classical minuets employ rounded two-reprise form. In addition, many of the opening themes of theme-and-variation sets and the initial refrain of rondos are cast in this design. In addition to several previous pieces in the text, such as Examples 22.9 and 22.13, consult the Beethoven minuets in Chapter 25 of the text and Chapter 23 of the Workbook, as well as the Mozart D Major theme and variations in the following section. The analysis project here utilizes the Scherzo and Trio from Beethoven's Piano Sonata in D Major, Op. 28. This movement not only features a number of diversions from the stereotypical two-reprise model but also exhibits several interesting relationships between the Scherzo and the Trio.

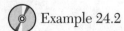 Example 24.2

BEETHOVEN: PIANO SONATA IN D MAJOR, OP. 28, III

SCHERZO
Allegro vivace

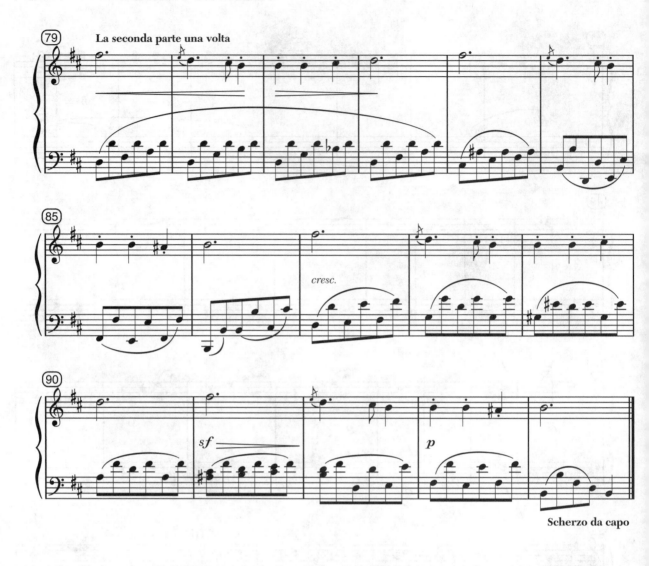

Scherzo da capo

The following movements may be used for further study.

Diabelli: Waltz in C Major.

Haydn: Symphony No. 104 in D Major ("London"), III. This movement has several interesting twists, such as the written-out repeat of the first reprise with altered orchestration, the humorous pause before the final four bars, and the foreign key of the Trio with the subsequent transition back to the da capo.

Mozart: Symphony No. 40 in G Minor, III. The use of rhythmic dissonance and phrase grouping is especially noteworthy here.

Ternary Form (ABA)

Examples of three-part form (ABA) may be found in many slow movements of the Classical period, some songs of Schubert, shorter waltzes, certain mazurkas by Chopin, and intermezzi by Brahms. One such piece is the Chopin F Major Mazurka shown in Example 24.3. In which church mode is the middle section cast? How would you answer the suggestion that this work is in rondo form?

Example 24.3

Chopin: Mazurka in F Major, Op. 68, No. 3

Allegro ma non troppo

Following are additional examples of Classical variation sets.

Mozart: Piano Sonata in A Major, K. 331, I. The theme of these charming variations has perhaps been analyzed to death.

Beethoven: Variations on "God Save the King," WoO 78. An inconsequential set but amusing because of the familiar theme; you might wish to compare this set to Charles Ives's Variations on the same tune.

Beethoven: Piano Sonata in A-flat Major, Op. 26, No. 1, I. An excellent example of Beethoven's early variation technique for piano.

Beethoven: Symphony No. 5 in C Minor, II. This freer handling of variation form uses two themes, of which only the first is varied.

Beethoven: "Diabelli" Variations in C Major for Piano, Op. 120. These thirty-two variations and closing double fugue represent the highest achievement in this technique. They are approached in stature only by Brahms's variations on themes by Haydn, Handel, and Paganini.

RONDO

Since the text contains a complete Haydn five-part rondo (Example 24.9), we will quote an example of Beethoven's use of the seven-part form—the last movement of his "Pathétique" Piano Sonata in C Minor, Op. 13. In addition to the movement's overall tonal scheme, examine the piece for transitions or bridges that link the various sections together. What is Beethoven's little joke at the very end of the work?

Example 24.6

BEETHOVEN: PIANO SONATA IN C MINOR ("PATHÉTIQUE"), OP. 13, III

Following are additional examples of rondo form.

Mozart: Piano Sonata in C Major, K. 545, III. A very condensed rondo
               form.
Haydn: Symphony No. 101 in D Major ("Clock"), IV. This movement
               contains some interesting modifications of the initial refrain.
Beethoven: Piano Sonata in G Major, Op. 49, No. 2, II. A model case of
               five-part rondo.
Beethoven: String Quartet in C Minor Op. 18, No. 4, IV. A textbook ex-
               ample of seven-part rondo.
               Two rondos from Romantic symphonies are cited below.
Tchaikovsky: Symphony No. 4 in F Minor, IV. The major-mode Finale is cast
               in rondo form; the first episode features a series of variations
               on a Russian folk tune.
Rachmaninoff: Symphony No. 2 in E Minor, II. This scherzo-like movement is
               a clear example of seven-part rondo design.

C H A P T E R   2 5

Two Analysis Projects

Two extensive passages are quoted below. The first is the initial Minuet from the third movement of Mozart's "Linz" Symphony No. 36 in C Major; the other is a complete figuration prelude from the Baroque period. Choose one of these and (1) make a voice-leading reduction, (2) provide a Roman numeral analysis, and (3) comment on the themes, motives, phrasing, texture, and so forth. In addition, address the issues that are raised in the directions for each excerpt.

1   The Minuet section of this symphony is cast in typical two-reprise form. However, there are several significant deviations from the usual design as diagramed in Chapters 24 and 25 of the text, which involve tonality, thematic material, and phrase grouping. Identify these deviations in your analysis.

 Example 25.1

Mozart: Symphony No. 36 in C Major ("Linz"), III, Minuet

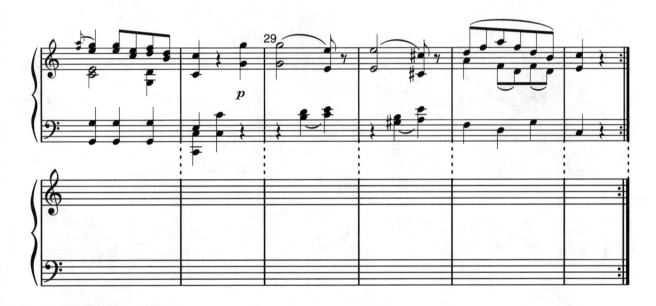

_____

_____

_____

_____

_____

2 The familiar C Major Prelude that opens the first volume of Bach's monumental *Well-Tempered Clavier* is actually a later revision of the original version. See the Kalmus edition for Hans Bischoff's comments on the earlier versions. The persistent sixteenth-note patterns shown here in the initial four measures continue throughout the remainder of the piece; in fact, this shorthand version is the way Bach originally notated the prelude.

The A^5 and G^5 in measures 5 and 7 momentarily cover the underlying stepwise soprano voice leading. Compare the tonal motion in measures 7–11 with that in measures 15–19. How are the two diatonic chords in measures 21 and 24 connected? What is the function of the passage in measures 24–31? Why do you think Bach resolves this section to a tonic triad with a $\flat\hat{7}$ (or V^7/IV)? Before you answer the last question, try playing the piece and resolve the chord in measure 31 to the last chord of the piece, skipping measures 32–33. After examining your analysis, you might wish to consult Heinrich Schenker's voice-leading graph of this prelude in his *Five Graphic Analyses* (New York: Dover, 1969).

 Example 25.2

BACH: PRELUDE IN C MAJOR FROM *THE WELL-TEMPERED CLAVIER*, BOOK I

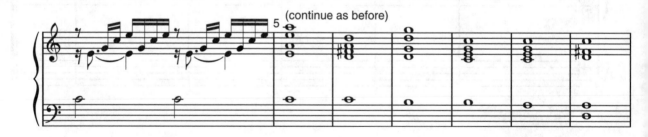

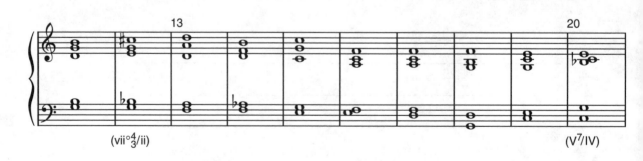

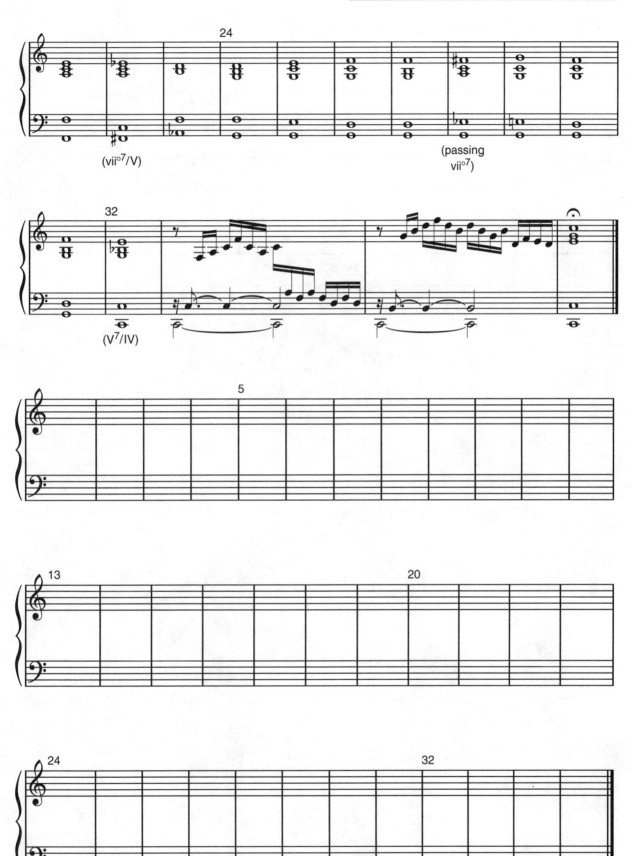

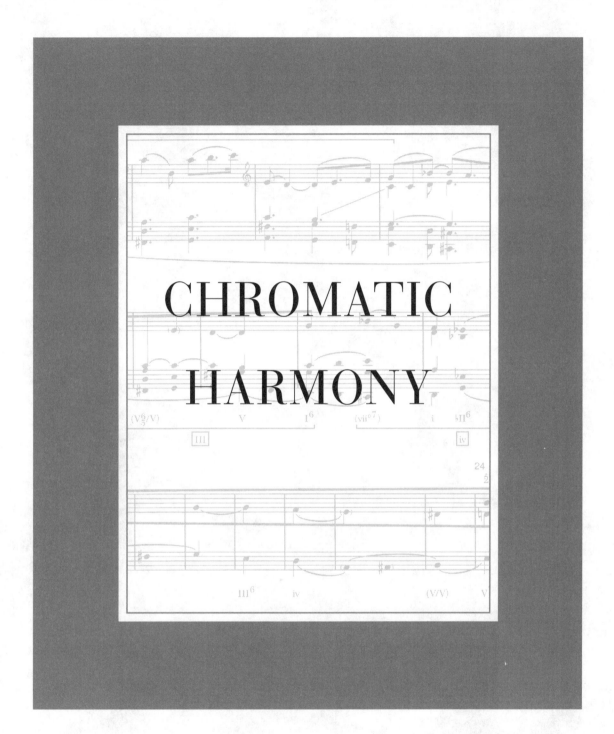

CHROMATIC

HARMONY

C H A P T E R   2 6

Review of Diatonic Harmony

Since Chapter 26 does not require student assignments, the following examples review the material in Chapters 9–25.

1 Compose original phrases in four-part texture that illustrate the chords or devices listed below. You may use chorale style or try more rhythmically varied textures. Be sure to stay within the indicated keys.

A. Use a V_5^6 chord and a cadential $_4^6$ in A major.

B. Use a $ii^{ø_3^4}$ chord and a 4-3 suspension in F minor.

C. Use a vi chord and modulate to $\boxed{V}$ from G major.

D. Use a $vii^{°_3^4}$ and end with a Phrygian cadence in B minor.

E. Use voice exchange and a passing $_4^6$ in D♭ major.

Example 26.1

2   The outer voices of the first section in a Mozart minuet for wind octet are quoted below. Examine them carefully and indicate how the two parts are related. _____ Is this relationship strict throughout? _____ To what key does this section of the minuet modulate? _____ Would you consider this key change normal for a first reprise in a minor mode?

_____

Using the figured-bass symbols that are supplied, add two middle parts to complete a four-voice texture. Since your tenor voice must be rather high in some places, you may wish to write it in the treble clef. Take care with your partwriting, as there are several tricky spots. Supply a Roman numeral analysis.

Example 26.2

MOZART: WIND SERENADE IN C MINOR, K.388, III

3 The passage that immediately follows the first reprise of the minuet in Example 26.2 is quoted below. Make a voice-leading reduction of this passage, omitting all unison doublings. What type of sequence is exemplified here? _____ _____ Which type of melodic dissonance does Mozart exploit? _____

Example 26.3

MOZART: WIND SERENADE IN C MINOR, K.388, III

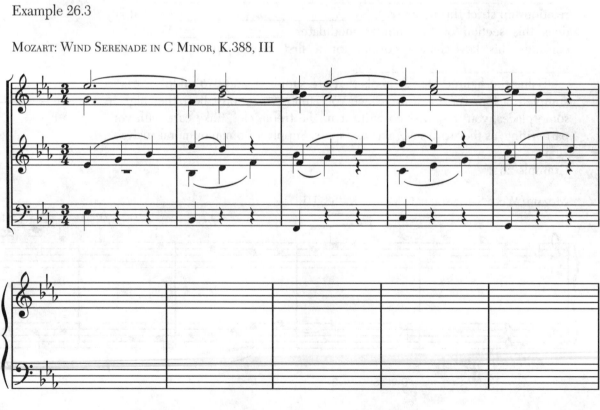

C H A P T E R   2 7

Tonicization and Modulation III:

MODULATION TO CLOSELY RELATED KEYS

1 Example 27.1 studies the functions of various triads in different keys and therefore shows how those triads can be used as pivot chords in modulations. In the first square, the top row lists the Roman numerals of diatonic triads in F major; the left-hand column shows tonicized new keys. In each column, indicate the function that triad will have in the new keys. The first column has been completed as a model. Then do the same thing for the triads in G minor in the second square.

Example 27.1

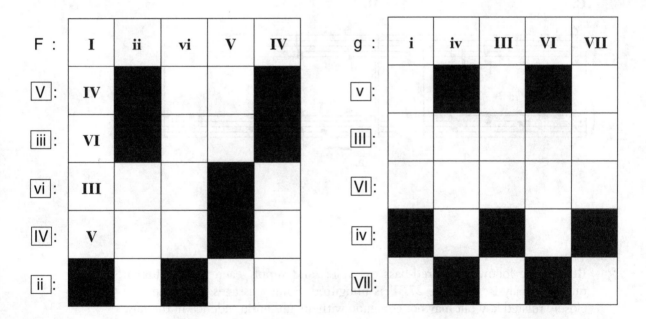

2 The following series of four-note progressions begin in the key indicated and make either a pivot-chord or chromatic modulation to a closely related key. Provide an appropriate Roman numeral analysis below each passage.

Example 27.2

A.

Eb:

B.

f#:

C.

F:

D.

b:

E.

G:

F.

c:

G.

E:

H.

a:

3 Realize the following figured-bass examples, and supply each with a Roman
numeral analysis. Example 27.3B is unfigured. Some passages modulate to a
closely related key but may not conclude with an authentic cadence in the new
key area. In those cases where the modulation occurs by chromaticism, a pivot
chord is not necessary.

Example 27.3

A.

B.

C.

D.

E.

4 The outer voices of a series of modulating progressions are given below. For each progression, determine the new closely related key area, which in most cases is reinforced by an authentic cadence. Since the bass line is not figured, you must first add appropriate figured-bass symbols, then provide a Roman numeral analysis. It is *not* necessary to fill in the alto and tenor voices. Be sure to indicate any pivot chords in terms of both keys. Several may change key through direct chromatic modulation.

Example 27.4

E.

F.

C:

Bb:

5 When harmonizing melodies of more than one phrase, it is important that you examine the different melodic formulas at the cadence points for possible modulations to closely related keys. Although these formulas may remain diatonic in the original key, their scale degrees will have a different melodic function in the new area. For instance, in C major the cadential notes E–D are scale steps $\hat{3}$-$\hat{2}$, implying a half cadence (I–V). But if you decide to modulate to D minor (or ⅱ), these same notes would function as scale steps $\hat{2}$-$\hat{1}$, implying a perfect authentic cadence.

Each pair of soprano notes given below likewise suggests more than one melodic cadence within the given key signatures. For example, you may wish to set Exercise 27.5A in either A major or F♯ minor. Fill in the missing voices and label the scale degrees and Roman numerals in each key.

Example 27.5

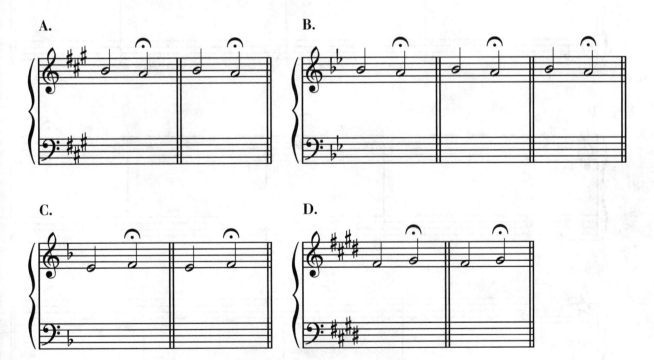

A.

B.

C.

D.

6 Make a four-voice setting of one of the melodies below. First examine the cadence tones in the melody for possible tonicizations or modulations. Try to incorporate some modulations to closely related keys. For example, the first melodic cadence in Example 27.6A might be an imperfect authentic cadence in F major ($\hat{2}$-$\hat{3}$ in the soprano) or a Phrygian cadence in D minor ($\hat{4}$-$\hat{5}$ in the soprano). Remember that the melody can return to the original key immediately following each key change and cadence. Supply a Roman numeral analysis.

Example 27.6

A. "DAS WALT' GOTT" (CHORALE TUNE)

F:

B.

c#:

7 Analyze the following excerpts, all of which modulate to a closely related key. In addition to supplying a Roman numeral analysis, provide a voice-leading reduction for Example 27.7C using the blank staves.

A. Does the progression in measures 4–5 constitute a modulation? _____
_____ Support your opinion. _____
_____

Example 27.7A

ALEXEI LVOV: "GOD SAVE THE CZAR" (FORMER RUSSIAN NATIONAL ANTHEM)

B. Even though the last chord of this passage omits the chordal 3rd, why is there no doubt about the mode of the new key? _____
_____

Example 27.7B

MOZART: WIND SERENADE IN C MINOR, K.388, IV

C. What type of sequence does Handel employ in measures 1–6 of his Minuet? _____

_____

Example 27.7C

HANDEL: MINUET IN F MAJOR

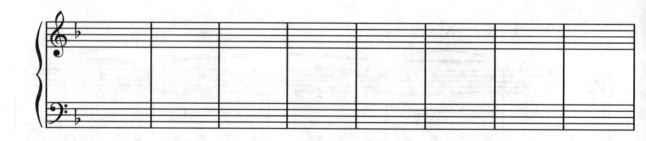

D. This hymn setting contains a number of brief shifts to closely related keys. Be sure that you align the symbols for the pivot chords and indicate the new key areas with a Roman numeral enclosed in a box.

Example 27.7D

"St. Matthew" (hymn tune)

E. This last excerpt features an extended tonicization of the minor dominant key ($\boxed{\text{v}}$), or E minor in terms of the original A major. Does a new secondary key area occur within this E minor section? _____ If so, what is its relationship to E minor? _____

Example 27.7E

BEETHOVEN: STRING QUARTET IN A MAJOR, OP. 18, NO. 5, I

(A) $\boxed{\text{v}}$:

CHAPTER 28

Modal Exchange and Mixture Chords

1 In the two-chord progressions in major keys in Example 28.1, one is a mixture chord. Supply the correct Roman numerals for both harmonies, following the model of the first example.

Example 28.1

2 Supply the indicated mixture chords in the following progressions, using a chord structure that connects smoothly to the harmonies that follow.

Example 28.2

3 Realize the following figured-bass exercises and provide a Roman numeral analysis for each. Note that Example 28.3E is unfigured.

Example 28.3

E.

4 A short piece in chorale style is given below. Examine it carefully, considering any possible modulations, and locate those chords that are likely candidates for mixture chords; not all will work equally well. Change their notation by adding one or more accidentals to produce appropriate mixture harmonies. Then provide a Roman numeral analysis of your finished product. Play the original and compare it with your altered version.

Example 28.4

5 Soprano lines have been provided for a series of short phrases. Write in the indicated mixture chord in each, then complete the remainder of the progression in four-voice texture. Be sure to include a Roman numeral analysis.

Example 28.5

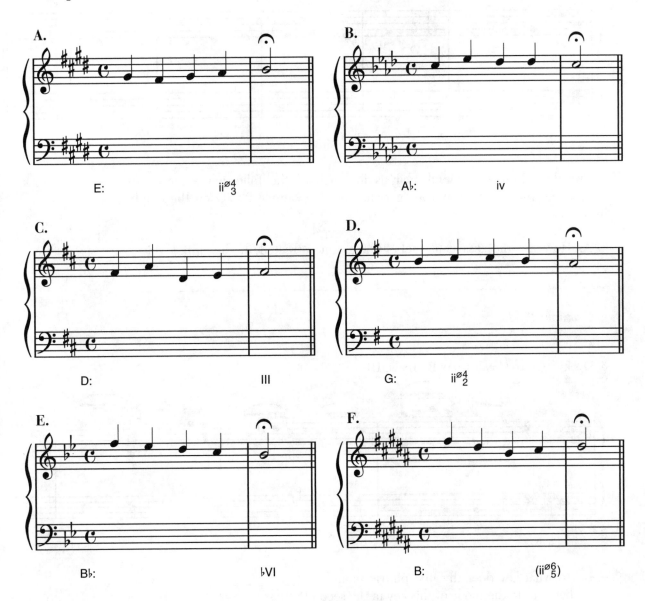

6. Provide a harmonization for the following melody. Use appropriate mixture chords for those notes marked with an arrow. Provide a Roman numeral analysis of your setting.

Example 28.6

7 Provide a Roman numeral analysis for each of the following excerpts. In addition, provide a voice-leading reduction of Example 28.7D on the empty staves.

A. How are the dissonant embellishing tones treated in the upper voice?

_____

_____

Example 28.7A

Dvořák: Cello Concerto in B Minor, III

B. To what key does the first phrase modulate? _____ What happens to the mode of this key in the second phrase? _____

_____

Example 28.7B

"National Hymn" (hymn)

C. Which mixture chord is prolonged in the famous operatic trio? _____

Example 28.7C

GOUNOD: TRIO FROM *FAUST*, ACT IV (SIMPLIFIED)

G:

D. Analyze this entire passage in terms of F major. What key is momentarily tonicized in measures 3–4? _____ How did Schubert manage to get from his original F major to this key and back to F major again?

_____

_____ Bracket the units of the soprano sequence that your reduction reveals.

Example 28.7D

SCHUBERT: WALTZ IN F MAJOR

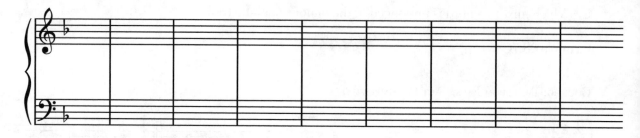

E. This kind of closing section has been called an extended plagal cadence. Which mixture chord extends the final plagal motion to I? _____

_____

Example 28.7E

BRAHMS: SYMPHONY NO. 3 IN F MAJOR, II

F. Example 28.7F quotes a setting of the famous "Kiss" motif from the Act I Love Duet of Verdi's *Otello*. This passage achieves much of its expressive power from the reiterated C♯ in the soprano line. Circle those C♯'s that are dissonant to the supporting chords; be careful in measure 5.

    This beautiful excerpt contains a number of secondary dominants. What is unusual about its only mixture chord? _____

_____

Example 28.7F

VERDI: LOVE DUET FROM *OTELLO*, ACT I

G. This sweeping passage provides an impetuous non-tonic opening to Strauss's portrait of this legendary libertine. What is the tonic? _____
_____ What is the first chord? _____
_____

Example 28.7G

RICHARD STRAUSS: *DON JUAN*

C H A P T E R   2 9

The Neapolitan Chord

1 Write out the Neapolitan chord in the following minor keys; the choice of soprano is up to you. While you should avoid doubling the ♭$\hat{2}$ in first and second inversions, you may double it in root-position chords. When spelling the ♭II triad in flat keys, be sure that you build it on the flatted second scale degree (C♭ E♭ G♭ in B♭ minor, not the enharmonic B D♯ F♯).

Example 29.1

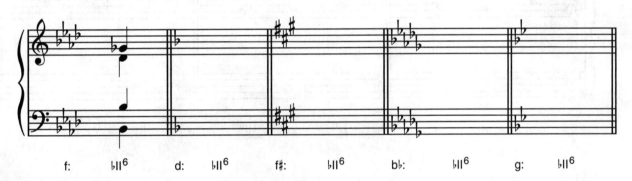

f: ♭II⁶   d: ♭II⁶   f♯: ♭II⁶   b♭: ♭II⁶   g: ♭II⁶

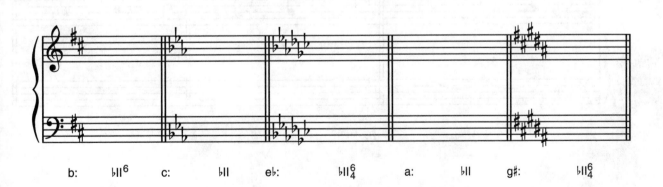

b: ♭II⁶   c: ♭II   e♭: ♭II$^6_4$ a: ♭II   g♯: ♭II$^6_4$

2   In the following three-chord progressions, the Roman numerals of the key and the soprano line are provided. Write the bass line, then fill in the inner voices, making sure that you spell the Neapolitan triad correctly.

Example 29.2

3 Realize the following figured-bass examples, and supply a Roman numeral
analysis for each. Although most of the Neapolitan chords in these examples
are cadential, several are found in embellishing progressions within the phrase.
Example 29.3A is unfigured.

Example 29.3

E.

F.

4 Write out cadential progressions for the following passages, employing an appropriate Neapolitan chord in each. Either the soprano or the bass is provided. In Examples 29.4B and 29.4C, incorporate the indicated chords into your settings.

Example 29.4

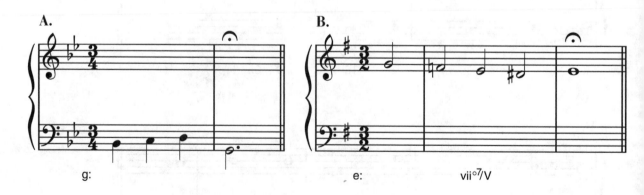

C.

D.

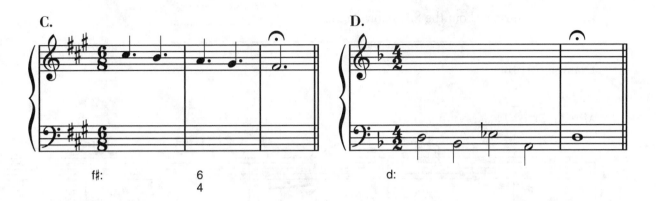

f#:   6
                       4

d:

5 Harmonize this melody, using at least two appropriate Neapolitan chords.

Example 29.5

e:

6 Provide a Roman numeral analysis of the short excerpts cited below.

A. How is the Neapolitan treated here? _____

_____

Example 29.6A

BRUCKNER: *CHRISTUS FACTUS EST* (TEXT OMITTED)

B. What is unusual about the first chord in measure 3? _____
_____

Example 29.6B

MOZART: STRING QUARTET IN D MINOR, K.421, IV

C. Assume the key is B minor; what creates a dissonant clash with the Neapolitan chord in measure 4? _____
What interval is emphasized here? _____ Why do you
think this interval is appropriate for this text? _____
_____

Example 29.6C

WAGNER: THE CURSE ON THE RING FROM *DAS RHEINGOLD*, SCENE 4

Wie durch Flucht er mir gerieth,   Since through a curse I gained it,
verflucht sei dieser Ring.   My curse lies on this ring.

D. Locate the ♭II. How is it tonicized? _____
Which harmony do you think is implied by the opening soprano note?
_____

Example 29.6D

Chopin: Mazurka in A Minor, Op. 7, No. 2

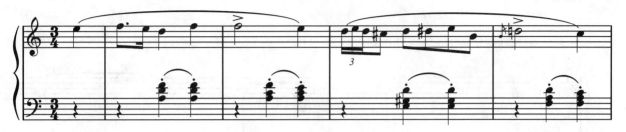

E. Why do you think Schubert momentarily changed the key signature in this
   passage? _____
   _____

Example 29.6E

Schubert: Moment Musical No. 6 in A-flat Major

F. What is peculiar about the Neapolitan chord in this excerpt? _____

_____

Example 29.6F

SCHUBERT: STRING QUARTET NO. 14 IN D MINOR ("DEATH AND THE MAIDEN"), I

(Ger$^6_5$)

G. What gives an additional bite to the ♭II harmony in measures 4–5? _____

_____

_____

_____

Example 29.6G

SAINT-SAËNS: _INTRODUCTION AND RONDO CAPRICCIOSO_

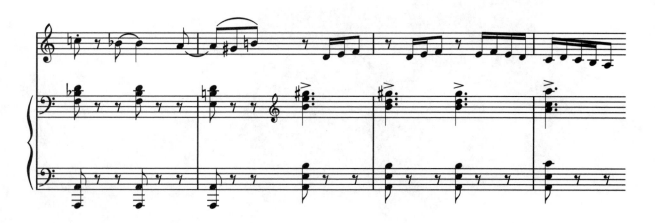

H. In this curious passage, why does the harmonic background in measure 2 seem at odds with the soprano line? _____

Name two different ways of harmonically analyzing this progression.
_____
_____

Example 29.6H

BEETHOVEN: PIANO SONATA IN C-SHARP MINOR ("MOONLIGHT"), OP. 27, NO. 2, I

C H A P T E R   3 0

Augmented Sixth Chords

1 A key and bass note have been provided in each example. For each bass note write an It^6, Fr$^4_3$, and Ger$^6_5$; you may choose your own soprano. Identify each augmented sixth below the staff.

Example 30.1

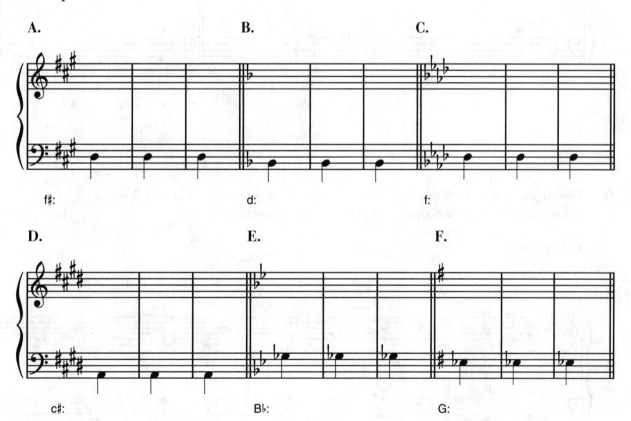

2 Approach and resolve the following augmented sixth chords in four-voice texture, using the Roman numeral labels that are supplied; watch for inversions. The soprano voice is given; the bass voice must be deduced from the Roman numerals and figured-bass symbols. The N and P above the staves denote neighboring and passing harmonies.

Example 30.2

A.

e: i   It^6 V

B.

g: i   Fr$^4_3$ V

C.

c#:   i   Ger$^6_5$ $^6_4$ $^5_3$
                        V

D.

c: i   Ger$^6_5$ V

E.

Eb: I   IV^6 It^6 V

F.

D: V   bVI   It^6 V

3 The augmented sixth chords in the progressions of Example 30.3 either resolve to harmonies other than V or appear in less common inversions.

Example 30.3

A.

G:

B.

d:

C.

Eb:

D.   **E.**   **F.**

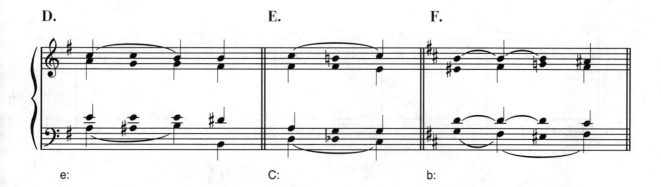

e: C: b:

4 Realize the figured-bass examples below and supply a Roman numeral analysis for each; Example 30.4 is unfigured. Be careful how you label and resolve the various augmented sixth chords.

Example 30.4

A.

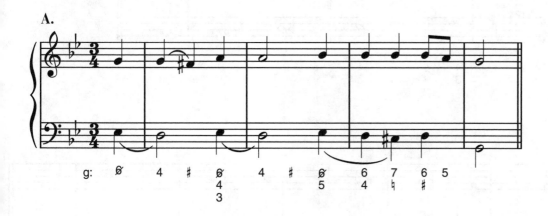

B.

C.

d: 6   7   6   ø   6   7   6   ø   ♯
   4   ♮   4   5   4   ♭   4   4
                                                   3

D.

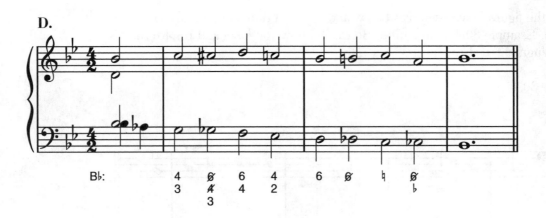

B♭:   4   ø   6   4   6   ø   ♮   ø
      3   4   4   2   ♭
               3

E.

e: 6   4   6   8   ø   6   5   ♯
           2   ♭7   5   4   ♯
                     3

F.

f♯:

5   Make a four-voice setting of the following tune, using appropriate augmented sixth chords on those notes marked with arrows. Although this tune begins and ends in C minor, it modulates into another key by measure 4; it is necessary to make this key shift in order to use a correct augmented sixth in measure 5.

Example 30.5

c:

6   Supply a Roman numeral analysis for these excerpts and provide voice-leading reductions for those passages followed by empty staves.

A. Locate, identify, and explain the derivation of the single augmented sixth chord in this enigmatic theme. _____
_____
_____

Example 30.6A

ELGAR: THEME FROM *ENIGMA VARIATIONS*

B. What voice-leading device does Mozart employ in this brief passage?

_____

_____

How would you indicate this device in your reduction? _____

_____

Example 30.6B

Mozart: Duel Scene from *Don Giovanni*, Act I

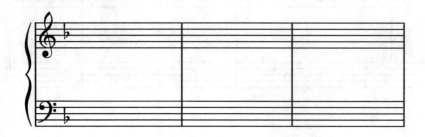

C. How is the listener misled at the opening of this charming Schumann waltz? _____

_____

_____

Example 30.6C

Schumann: "Waltz" from *Albumblätter*

D. In the reduction given below, which two chords immediately precede the final tonic? _____
What do we call this harmonic relationship? _____

Example 30.6D

WAGNER: OVERTURE TO *TANNHÄUSER*

E:

E. In this passage Brahms uses an augmented sixth chord in the process of making a modulation from A minor to C major ([i] to [III]). How does this affect the resolution of the augmented sixth chord? _____
_____

Example 30.6E

BRAHMS: INTERMEZZO IN A MINOR, OP. 118, NO. 1

a:

7 The passage from Schumann's "Die beiden Grenadiere" ("The Two Grenadiers") quoted in Example 30.7 makes extensive use of augmented sixth chords. Make a Roman numeral analysis and voice-leading reduction. There are two different ways of viewing the tonal structure of this section; you may wish to discuss the merits of each in class.

Example 30.7

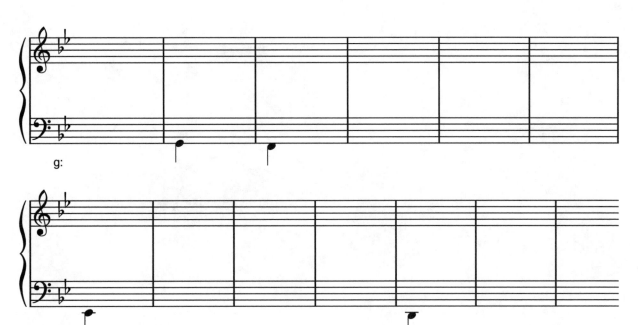

g:

C H A P T E R 3 1

Complex Forms

Like its counterpart, Chapter 24 in the Workbook, this chapter provides several pieces or movements for formal and tonal analysis and suggests additional works for further study.

SONATA FORM

This Piano Sonata in C Major, K. 309, dates from Mozart's visit to Mannheim, where he was undoubtedly influenced by the innovations initiated by the famous orchestra there. The opening of the first movement, cited here, employs the call and response of the Galant style, which in orchestral music alternated *forte* and *piano* passages. Although Mozart's treatment of sonata form is fairly conventional here, there are a few unusual features of the movement that you may want to highlight.

 Example 31.1

MOZART: PIANO SONATA IN C MAJOR, K.309, I

Additional works for analysis:

Clementi: Piano Sonata in D Major, Op. 36, No. 6, I.

Haydn: Symphony No. 100 in G Major ("Military"), I. After the lengthy introduction, this movement is an excellent example of monothematic sonata form.

Mozart: Piano Sonatas in D Major, K. 311, and in C Major, K. 545, I. The first movements of these two sonatas feature unusual thematic or tonal procedures in their recapitulations.

Beethoven: String Quartet in F Major, Op. 18, No. 1, I. The insistence on the opening motive influences the rest of the thematic material in this movement.

Beethoven: Symphony No. 5 in C Minor, I. This movement concludes with an extended coda that appears to introduce a new theme. Peter Schickele's hilarious and insightful "Bob and Ray" football commentary should not be missed.

The opening movements of the Beethoven Piano Sonatas in D Minor, Op. 31, No. 2 ("Tempest") and C Major, Op. 53 ("Waldstein") contain some interesting deviations from conventional sonata form. Either might form the basis for an extended analytical paper.

Brahms: Rhapsody in G Minor, Op. 79, No. 2. The development is based largely on the principal and closing themes. Does Brahms employ the traditional key relationships?

CONCERTO FORM

The length of most concerto first movements prohibits their quotation here. Following are several works for possible analysis.

Mozart: Concerto for Flute in G Major, K. 285c, I. A very conventional concerto form.

Mozart: Concerto for Clarinet in A Major, K. 622, I. Mozart's last piece in this genre and one of his greatest concertos.

Mozart: Concerto for Piano in D Minor, K. 466, I. This dark-hued movement in symphonic style contains a number of unusual features.

Beethoven: Concerto for Piano in C Minor, Op. 37, I. Although the design is fairly traditional, Beethoven's constant employment of motives drawn from the opening theme is innovative.

Chopin: Concerto for Piano in F Minor, I. While the piano writing is definitely Romantic, the design of this movement is surprisingly Classical. There is no cadenza.

Brahms: Violin Concerto in D Major, I. Despite the late date of this work (1878), it displays all of the usual structural attributes of a Classical concerto. However, the secondary theme is missing in the opening orchestral tutti (T1).

SONATA-RONDO FORM

Following are examples of this form for analysis.

Mozart: Concerto for Piano in B-flat Major, K. 450, III. The handling of the form is fairly conventional here; note the amusing Turkish ending. Mozart uses the sonata-rondo in many of his other piano concertos; some, like the D minor listed above, omit the third refrain, resulting in what has been termed a "binary rondo."

Mozart: Piano Sonata in B-flat Major, K. 333, III. Curiously enough, this delightful movement displays certain concerto features, including a full-fledged cadenza.

Beethoven: Piano Sonata in E-flat Major, Op. 27, No. 1, ("Quasi una fanta-sia"), III. Almost a textbook example of this form.

Beethoven: Concerto for Piano in E-flat Major, Op. 73, III. In this lengthy sonata-rondo, the second refrain is slighted as it leads into the development, which is largely based on three statements of the principal theme in an unusual key relationship. There is a typical slowdown immediately preceding the final burst of energy in the last thirteen measures.

CHORALE PRELUDE

Johann Walther (1684–1748) was an important figure in the development of the Baroque organ chorale prelude, as evidenced by the careful attention J. S. Bach paid to his works. In this short piece, the cantus appears in the bass voice, a practice that severely restricts the scope of harmonic possibilities; note the limited number of modulations. What relationship do the upper voices bear to each other? Why do you think this procedure is rendered even more difficult by the presence of preexisting chorale tune? You may wish to make some voice-leading diagrams of the cantus passages, observing any typical sequential patterns.

 Example 31.2

JOHANN WALTHER: VERS 2 OF "ACH GOTT UND HERR"

Additional works for analysis:

Bach: "Wachet auf" (Schübler Chorales for organ). This famous piece originally appeared in Cantata No. 140 ("Wachet auf") as a movement for tenors and strings. The recurrence of the opening material gives the work a ritornello effect.

Bach: "Jesu, Joy of Man's Desiring." The initial triplet theme of this familiar work is actually derived from the first phrase of the cantus.

Bach: "Vor deinen Thron tret' ich." Despite the myth that Bach dictated this work on his deathbed, this piece was actually written earlier. Some have claimed that the number of notes in the cantus bear a numerological relationship to Bach's name.

INVENTION

Some background information on the Bach Inventions appears in Chapter 12 of the Workbook. Although the B minor Two-Part Invention appeared as No. 15 in Bach's published version of the *Clavierbüchlein*, it occurred near the middle of his original version, where it served to introduce the device of imitation in the dominant key.

 Example 31.3

BACH: TWO-PART INVENTION IN B MINOR

Additional works for analysis:

Bach: Two-Part Invention in F Major. This familiar little piece begins as a strict canon at the octave before moving to the dominant key. A transposed version of this same material occurs at the end.

Bach: Two-Part Invention in G Minor. A highly ingenious work that features double counterpoint and mirror writing. The latter part of the piece is a nearly complete transposition of the first half a perfect 5th lower.

Bach: Three-Part Invention in D Major. A classic example of triple counterpoint, in which the rearrangement of the voices follows a cyclical pattern.

FUGUE

Bach's important organ fugues are seldom analyzed; unfortunately, their length prohibits quotation here. The G minor fugue from Bach's *Well-Tempered Clavier* Vol. I offers some interesting features as well as several standard contrapuntal devices.

 Example 31.4

BACH: FUGUE IN G MINOR (*THE WELL-TEMPERED CLAVIER*, VOL. 1)

Additional works for analysis:

Handel: "And with His Stripes We Are Healed" from *Messiah*. One of the few choruses in this oratorio that is in strict fugal style; it maintains the same countersubject throughout.

Bach: Fugue in C Minor (*Well-Tempered Clavier*, Vol. 1). Although this piece has been analyzed to death, many commentators fail to mention the debt it owes to invertible counterpoint (double at the octave and twelfth as well as triple) and the interrelationships of its overall design.

Bach: Fugue in D-sharp Minor (*Well-Tempered Clavier*, Vol. 1). Probably the most complex three-voice fugue Bach ever wrote, a virtual encyclopedia of contrapuntal devices. The tonal scheme of its large three-part design is curious in its insistence on the tonic key.

Mozart: Kyrie from the *Requiem* in D Minor. This double fugue has a decided Handelian flavor; one of its subjects is very similar to "And with His Stripes," quoted above.

Haydn: String Quartet in F Minor, Op. 20, No. 2, IV. In another double fugue based on the same tune, Haydn puts the primary subject through its paces, including all the usual devices. A comparison of the Handel, Mozart, and Haydn would make an interesting paper.

C H A P T E R   3 2

Embellishing Chromatic Chords

1 Several of the embellishing harmonies in this chapter involve new chord types, such as the augmented triad (I^+) and the two altered dominant seventh chords ($V+^7$ and Vo^7) in which the chordal fifth is raised or lowered. Write the indicated sonorities on the treble staff, using the first example as a model.

Example 32.1

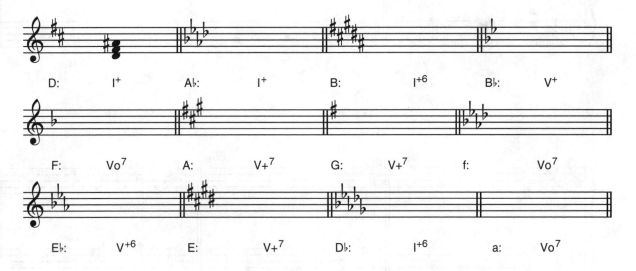

2 The key, Roman numerals, bass line, and first chord are provided in the following three-chord progressions. Write in the indicated embellishing harmony, making sure that the partwriting of the middle harmony connects smoothly with the chords that precede and follow it. The first one is done for you. Watch your spelling of the embellishing chromatic chords.

Example 32.2

J.   **K.**   **L.**

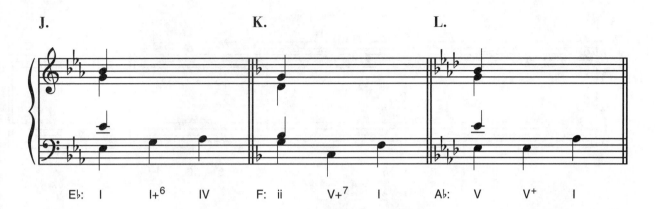

Eb: I   I+^{6} IV   F: ii   V+^{7} I   Ab: V   V$^+$ I

M.

G: ii   Vo^7 I

3   Realize the following figured-bass examples and supply a Roman numeral analysis. Be careful of the partwriting in Example 32.3A. Example 32.3D contains a variety of less common chromatic chords. You must supply your own soprano in Example 32.3E.

Example 32.3

A.

4 **A.** Employing the empty staves below and assuming the key of C major, use the diminished seventh chord D♯ F♯ A C in the following functions; employ a minimum of three chords for each progression.
1. a secondary vii°⁷
2. an embellishing neighboring chord
3. an embellishing passing chord

Example 32.4A

B. Now in the key of A major, employ the Ger6th F A C D♯ in each of the following functions.
1. a normal Ger$^6_5$
2. an embellishing neighboring chord
3. an embellishing passing chord

Example 32.4B

C. Write out authentic cadences in two keys of your choice, using four-voice texture. Employ a V°⁷ in one and a V+⁷ in the other. Be careful about the partwriting and the resolution of the augmented sixths or diminished thirds.

Example 32.4C

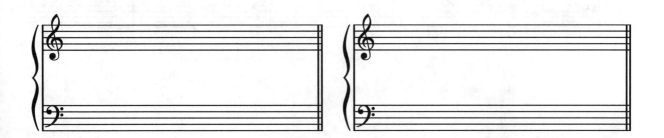

5 Make a four-voice harmonic setting for one of the tunes below. Use an appropriate embellishing chromatic chord for each note marked with an arrow. Provide a Roman numeral analysis.

Example 32.5

A.

B.

6 Provide a Roman numeral analysis for the following excerpts. For Examples 32.6A and 32.6C, make a voice-leading reduction in the empty staves.

A. Explain the harmony in measure 2. _____

_____

Example 32.6A

Dvořák: Symphony No. 9 in E Minor ("New World"), II

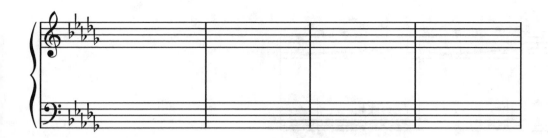

B. Observe how the embellishing chords allow a chromatic ascent in the vocal line from G♯⁴ to C♯⁵. What is the missing chordal member on beat 2 of the second measure? _____ Spell the entire chord. _____

Example 32.6B

Schubert: "Täuschung" from *Winterreise*

List,   die hin-ter Eis und Nacht __ und Graus __ ihm weist __

C. Use a five-voice texture for your voice-leading reduction, three in the treble clef and two in the bass clef. You may wish to lower the upper voices by an octave. How does the function of the embellishing chord in measure 2 differ from that in measure 5? _____ _____ What happens in the outer parts during this passage? _____ What is the basic function of this passage? _____ _____

Example 32.6C

Tchaikovsky: Waltz from *Sleeping Beauty*, Act I

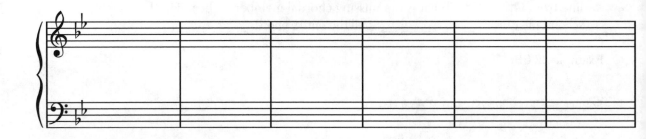

D. Fanny Hensel employs an embellishing harmony in the coda of her lovely song. What does she do to emphasize or highlight this chord? _____

_____

Example 32.6D

FANNY HENSEL: "MORGENSTÄNDCHEN" No. 5

E. How do the embellishing harmonies function in this famous aria? _____
_____

Example 32.6E

BIZET: MICAELA'S ARIA FROM *CARMEN*, ACT III

las,   que je re - ponds _ de moi;   mais   j'ai

F. Explain the two different ways in which these short passages from
Rachmaninoff's familiar Prelude treat the ♭2̂ in the upper voice. _____
_____
_____

Example 32.6F

RACHMANINOFF: PRELUDE IN C-SHARP MINOR, OP. 3, NO. 2

C H A P T E R   3 3

Dominant Prolongation

1 The following excerpts contain various dominant prolongations that occur in different formal contexts. Analyze each passage to determine the methods by which this harmony is extended. Supply voice-leading reductions for those exercises where empty staves have been provided.

A. In this lengthy retransition from a Haydn minuet, a variety of harmonies occurs over a dominant pedal in the first eight measures. What happens in measures 8–13? _____

_____

Example 33.1A

HAYDN: SYMPHONY NO. 100 IN G MAJOR ("MILITARY"), III

B. Explain the different ways in which these two passages prolong a cadential $^6_4$ before its eventual resolution to the tonic. (MacDowell) _____

_____

_____

(Verdi) _____

_____

_____

Example 33.1B

EDWARD MACDOWELL: "UNCLE REMUS" FROM *WOODLAND SKETCHES*

VERDI: "MISERERE" FROM *IL TROVATORE*, ACT IV

cor, il ____   re - spi - ro, i ____

pal -   pi -   ti ____ al ____ cor.

C. The opening sixteen measures of this Chopin waltz provide an introduction to the main theme. What does your voice-leading reduction reveal about how the dominant harmony is prolonged in measures 3–4 and 7–8? _____

_____

_____

Example 33.1C

Chopin: *Grande Valse Brilliante* in A-flat Major, Op. 34

D. This magnificent dominant prolongation immediately precedes the raising of the curtain on the final festive scene of Wagner's *Die Meistersinger*. As in the Haydn minuet (Example 33.1A), a variety of chords occur over an extended dominant pedal, but here the harmonies are considerably more complex; in fact, many of them seem to function as altered passing chords. Notice how the upper voice makes an overall stepwise diatonic descent, which is later joined by a falling chromatic line in the middle part in the third measure.

Example 33.1D

WAGNER: INTRODUCTION TO ACT III, SCENE 5, OF *DIE MEISTERSINGER*

2 The return of the opening theme of a minuet in Classical style is given below. In the blank measures, compose a retransition leading to this thematic material that contains a dominant prolongation. Try to retain the same style and perhaps utilize some of the motivic ideas.

Example 33.2

C H A P T E R   3 4

Modulation to Foreign Keys I

1 **A.** Assume you are making a modulation from the given key to the foreign key aligned directly below it. In Example 34.1A, supply an appropriate common tone and indicate its scale-degree function in both keys; follow the model of the first example.

Example 34.1A

Ab:	C = $\hat{3}$	G:		E:		Bb:	
III :	C = $\hat{1}$	VI :		bVI :		bIII	

c:		d:	
#iii :		bII :	

B. In Example 34.1B, supply an appropriate pivot or common chord. Follow the model of the first example.

Example 34.1B

Eb:	V/ii	A:		b:		F:	
III :	IV	VI		bII :		bVI	

B:		Db:	
bIII :		vii	

2 The following five-chord progressions modulate from the original key to a foreign key. Analyze each passage with Roman numerals. The pivot or common chord is usually an altered harmony in one of the two keys.

Example 34.2

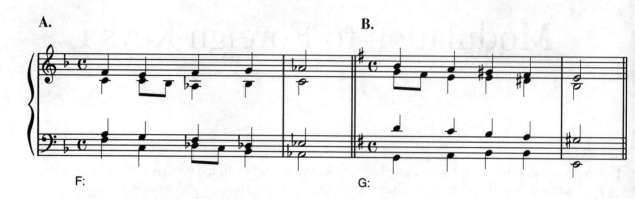

A.

F:

B.

G:

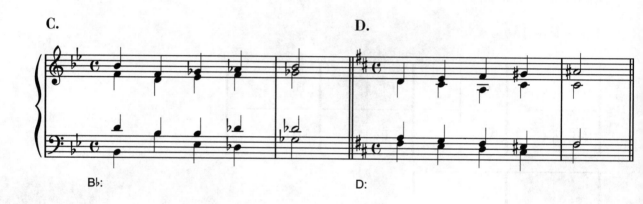

C.

B♭:

D.

D:

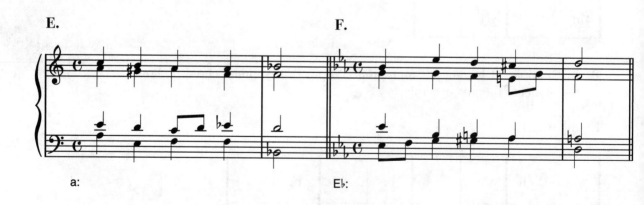

E.

a:

F.

E♭:

3 Realize the following figured-bass examples and provide a Roman numeral analysis. Each passage employs at least one modulation to a foreign key. In the space provided, name the type of modulation used—pivot chord, change of mode, or common tone.

Example 34.3

A.

B.

C.

D.

4 Provide a Roman numeral analysis of the following excerpts, indicating the original key, the new key, and the means of modulation.

A. Schubert's song "Die Sterne" ("The Stars") explores a number of foreign keys in rapid succession, all related by chromatic third to the original tonic of E♭ major. Indicate on the score the scale degrees that are used as common tones to link the two keys in each modulation.

Example 34.4A

Schubert: "Die Sterne," Op. 96, No. 1

B. The key signature here is misleading; it refers to the original tonic of
F minor (the clarinet part is notated at concert pitch). Determine the key
center in measures 1–6, the new key in measures 7–8, and the means of
modulation.

Example 34.4B

BRAHMS: CLARINET SONATA NO. 1 IN F MINOR, OP. 120, NO. 1

C. Notice that Verdi notates the new key enharmonically. Is there a common tone between the two keys, and if so, what is it? _____

_____

Example 34.4C

VERDI: TRIUMPHAL MARCH FROM *AIDA*, ACT I

D. The passage cited from this popular song forms a modulatory link between the end of its chorus (mm. 1–2) and the beginning of its bridge (mm. 3–7). Explain the difference between the original first three measures (No. 1) and the recomposed version of these measures (No. 2). _____

_____

_____

Example 34.4D

JEROME KERN: "THE WAY YOU LOOK TONIGHT"

E. This passage represents the link between the first and second sections in the slow movement of Mahler's "Titan" Symphony. What are the two keys, and what is the common tone between them? _____ _____ In the light of other common-tone modulations, what is unusual about this one? _____ _____

Example 34.4E

MAHLER: SYMPHONY NO. 1 IN D MAJOR, III

F. This striking quotation includes two transient tonicizations. Is either temporary tonic closely related to the original key of E major? _____ _____ How is the transition back to the original key effected? _____ _____

Example 34.4F

BERLIOZ: *HAROLD IN ITALY*, II

5 Compose three original passages employing a foreign modulation from a designated key. Use the indicated modulatory technique; the choice of texture is up to you.

A. B♭ major to $\boxed{\text{VI}}$ (G major), by common tone

Example 34.5A

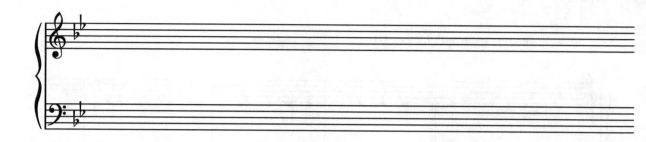

B. E major to $\boxed{\flat\text{III}}$ (G major), by change of mode

Example 34.5B

C. A♭ major to $\boxed{\text{VII}}$ (G major), by altered pivot chord

Example 34.5C

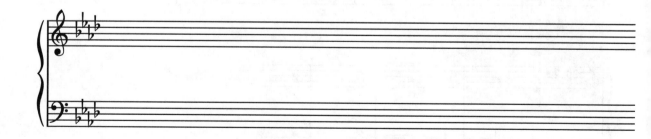

CHAPTER 35

Ninth, Eleventh, Thirteenth, and Added-Note Chords

1 Write the indicated ninth chords on the treble or bass staff; the first one will serve as a model. If you are not sure about the commercial symbols, refer to Chapter 35 or Appendix 4 in the text. Make sure that you distinguish between a Cm⁹ (C E♭ G B♭ D) and a C⁻⁹ (C E G B♭ D♭).

Example 35.1

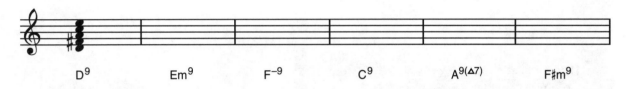

D⁹   Em⁹   F⁻⁹   C⁹   A⁹⁽ᐃ⁷⁾   F♯m⁹

B♭⁻⁹   Gm⁹   A♭⁹⁽ᐃ⁷⁾   E♭⁻⁹   C♯⁹   D⁹⁽ᐃ⁷⁾

2 Realize the figured-bass examples in four-voice texture. Leave out the chordal 5th in all ninth chords.

Example 35.2

A.

3 Write the following eleventh, thirteenth, and added-note chords on the treble or bass staff. Spell the complete chord in each case, including all chordal members.

Example 35.3

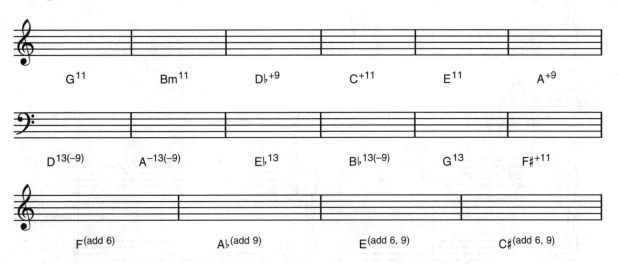

G^{11} Bm^{11} $D\flat^{+9}$ C^{+11} E^{11} A^{+9}

$D^{13(-9)}$ $A^{-13(-9)}$ $E\flat^{13}$ $B\flat^{13(-9)}$ G^{13} $F\#^{+11}$

$F^{(add\ 6)}$ $A\flat^{(add\ 9)}$ $E^{(add\ 6,\ 9)}$ $C\#^{(add\ 6,\ 9)}$

4 On the following staves, the key, some type of ninth or eleventh chord, and a soprano note are supplied. Make a five-voice setting of each progression; beware of parallels. Resolve the chordal 9th or 11th stepwise; the approach should use a neighboring (N), suspension (S), or appoggiatura (APP) figure, as specified.

Example 35.4

A.   **B.**

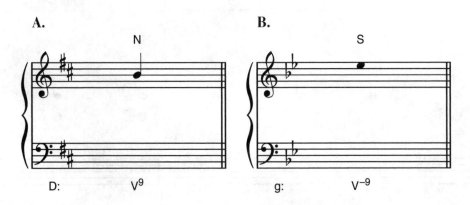

D: V^9 g: V^{-9}

C.

E: V⁹/V

D.

E♭:   V¹¹
(omit 3)

E.

b♭:   V⁻⁹

F.

A: V⁷ V⁹   I

G. (FIVE VOICES)

F: I   ii⁹   V⁹   I
              (add 6) (add 6
                       and 9)

H. (FIVE VOICES)

C: V⁻¹³⁽⁻⁹⁾/ii   V⁹/V   V⁻¹³⁽⁻⁹⁾   I⁹/△⁷

5 A harmonic progression has been indicated with commercial chord symbols. Write out the bass line in the empty measures and provide the correct Roman numerals. What familiar progression lies at the basis of this passage? _____

_____

Example 35.5

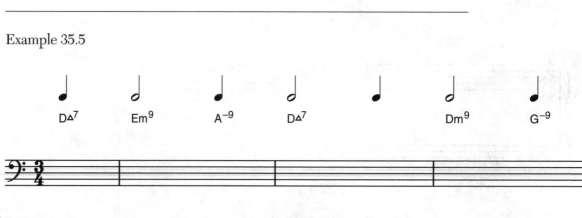

D△⁷   Em⁹   A⁻⁹   D△⁷   Dm⁹   G⁻⁹

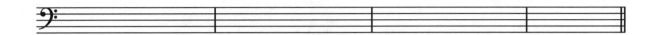

$C^{9(\triangle 7)}$ Cm^9 $F^{9(\triangle 7)}$ $B\flat m^9$ $E\flat^{\triangle 7}$ A^{-9} $D^{\triangle 7}$

6 Provide a Roman numeral analysis of the following excerpts and a voice-leading reduction for those passages supplied with blank staves.

A. In working out the soprano line in your reduction, you may want to disregard the G^5's in measures 2 and 4. Also consider the possibility of octave displacement in measure 6. What can you say about the upper voice in your final reduction? _____

Example 35.6A

JOHANN STRAUSS, JR.: *WINE, WOMEN, AND SONG* (WALTZ)

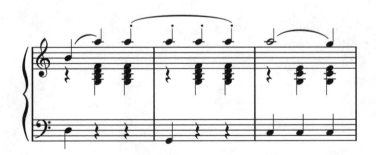

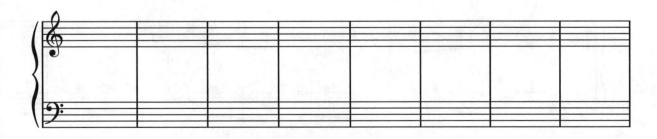

B. Notice that both the V^9 and V^{-9} are employed in this dominant prolongation. After making your reduction of this passage, state how the chordal 9ths are approached. _____

Example 35.6B

BEETHOVEN: PIANO SONATA IN B-FLAT MAJOR, OP. 22, III

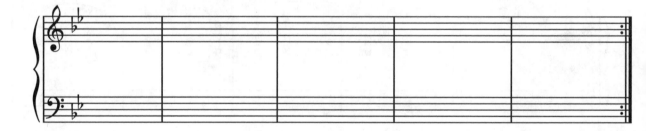

C. What are the two surprise notes in the amusing little passage? _____
_____ The upper voice actually consists of a compound melody made up of two separate lines. Can you explain the derivation of the curious dissonance in the fourth measure? _____
_____

Example 35.6C

BEETHOVEN: ECOISSAISE IN G MAJOR, WoO 23

D. The opening of this lovely song contains a variety of ninth chords. What is the familiar sequence that underlies this passage? _____

_____

Example 35.6D

Fauré: "Après un rêve," Op. 7, No. 1

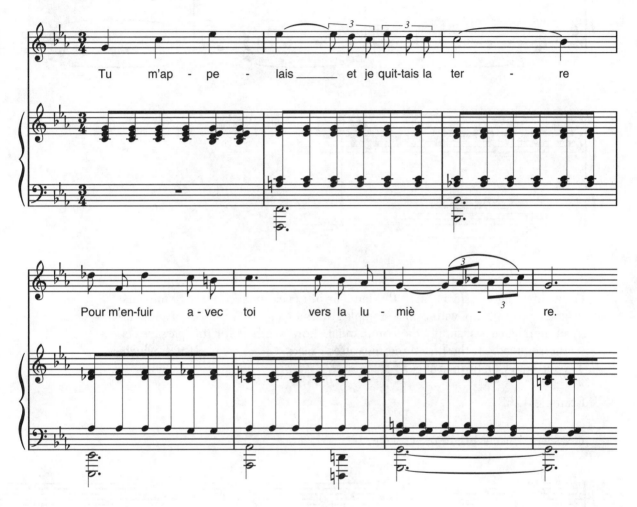

E. The underlying dominant harmony in this beguiling Rhinemaiden music is ornamented not only with chromatic embellishments but with ninth and eleventh chords as well.

How would you explain the D in the last chord? _____

_____

_____

Example 35.6E

WAGNER: RHINEMAIDENS' SCENE FROM *GÖTTERDÄMMERUNG*, ACT III

F. In this song Gershwin takes the familiar 5th cycle of secondary dominants and spices it up with some complex harmonies. In place of a Roman numeral analysis, supply the commercial chord symbols for this passage. Is the sequence in the first three measures exact? _____ If not, which chord did Gershwin change? _____

Example 35.6F

GERSHWIN: "NICE WORK IF YOU CAN GET IT"

C H A P T E R   3 6

Implication and Realization

1 A short composition from Schumann's collection of piano pieces for children is quoted below. As you play or listen to it on CD-ROM, trace how the composer continually uses a standard or normative progression to set up a sense of harmonic and melodic expectations, only to substitute an unexpected resolution or continuation at the last moment. Try playing the chords that you expect, then play Schumann's actual version.

In addition to providing a Roman numeral analysis of this piece, make a voice-leading reduction in the empty staves that are provided. In what way do the quasi-cadences in measures 2 and 4 parallel those in measures 6 and 8?

_____

In terms of A minor, what other harmonic function is possible in measure 9?

_____

Notice the $\hat{3}$-$\hat{2}$-$\hat{1}$ line in the opening melody. The final phrase is internally extended by two measures. What is the relationship of this extension to the cadential $^6_4$ that begins in measure 15? _____

How is this $^6_4$ related to the one in measure 17, which ushers in the final $\hat{3}$-$\hat{2}$-$\hat{1}$ resolution in the soprano? _____

 Example 36.1

Schumann: "★₊★" from *Album for the Young*, Op. 68, No. 21

Langsam und mit Ausdruck zu spielen

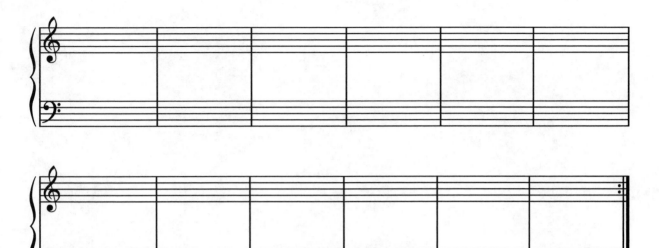

Harmonic Sequences III:

CHROMATIC ELABORATIONS OF DIATONIC SEQUENCES

1 The following two passages feature descending chromatic tetrachords. Set the passages differently in four-voice texture and supply an appropriate analysis with either figured-bass symbols or Roman numerals.

Example 37.1

A.

B.

2 Realize the following figured-bass examples and provide an appropriate analysis for each. Use Roman numerals for the beginning and ending of the patterns and figured-bass symbols for the interior sequential motion.

Example 37.2

A.

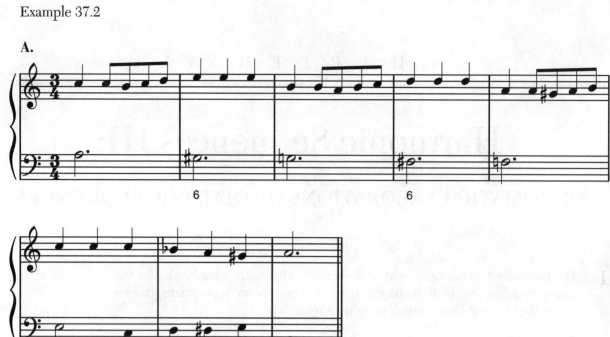

6   6

6   ♭6   7   ♯
           ♯

B.

6   4   3   6   4   3   6   ♮4   3   6   4   3
5   5   ♭5   5
            ♯

C.

5   6   7   4   ♭7   4   6   ♯
            ♭   ♭5   ♭   ♭5

3   For the following two passages, realize the figured-bass symbols in the first one and a half measures in four-voice texture. Then continue the sequence marked by the brackets and provide a conclusion or cadence for each example. Provide Roman numerals for the framing chords in each passage.

Example 37.3

A.

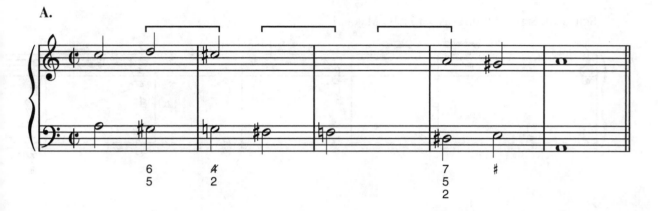

B.

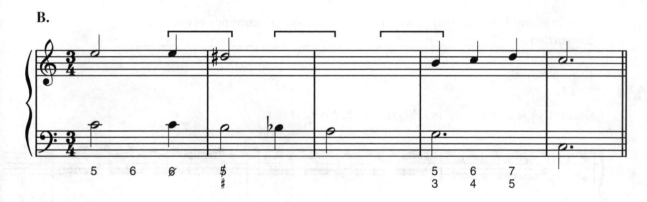

4   Supply an appropriate analysis for the following excerpts and identify each type of chromatic sequence in the blank lines. Provide voice-leading reductions for those examples that have empty staves.

A. _____

This passage is best understood if you read or play it backwards.

Example 37.4A

HANDEL: "O FATAL CONSEQUENCE OF RAGE" FROM *SAUL*, ACT II

B. _____

Why do you think a $^6_4$ chord was substituted for the expected sequential harmony in measure 6? _____

_____

Example 37.4B

SCHUBERT: STRING QUARTET NO. 15 IN G MAJOR, I

C. _____

Assuming the key is F major, why is it not feasible to continue this sequence any further? _____

Example 37.4C

CORELLI: CONCERTO GROSSO IN F MAJOR, OP. 6, NO. 6, II

D. _____

What unusual type of triad plays a significant role in this harmonic sequence?

_____

Why is the final chord unexpected compared with that in measure 3? _____

_____

Example 37.4D

CHOPIN: ETUDE IN A-FLAT MAJOR FROM *TROIS NOUVELLE ÉTUDES*

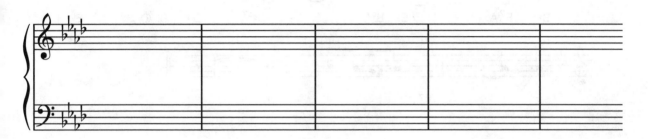

E. _____

Assuming the key is C minor, what is the harmonic function of the last chord?
_____

How does it result from the sequential motion? _____
_____

Example 37.4E

ALESSANDRO SCARLATTI: FUGUE IN F MINOR

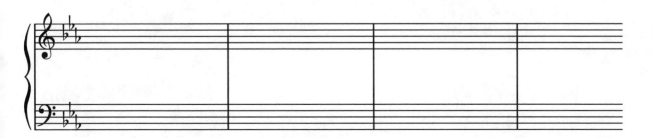

From the given tune and accompanying commercial chord symbols, provide a two-voice sequential framework in the provided staves and beam the underlying diatonic stepwise motion in the outer parts. Then provide a Roman numeral analysis.

Example 37.4F

RAY HENDERSON: "THE BIRTH OF THE BLUES"

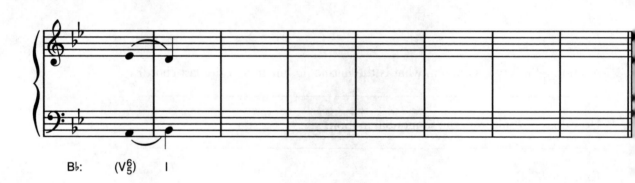

G. _____

What is the root movement between these tonicized harmonies? The passage begins in F♯ minor. _____
This excerpt is similar in nature to the Love Duet from *Tristan* quoted as Example 40.1 of the text.

Example 37.4G

Gounod: Love Duet from *Roméo et Juliette*, Act IV

jour! _____ Vois ces ray - ons ja - loux _____

dont l'ho - ri - zon se do - - re; De la nuit les flam-beaux pâ -

lis - sent, et l'au - ro - - re

C H A P T E R   3 8

An Analysis Project

1 The opening section of Isolde's final aria from *Tristan* is quoted below. Although we know it as the "Liebestod" ("Love-death"), a title that was later bestowed by Franz Liszt, it was originally entitled "Verklärung" ("Transfiguration") by Wagner, since the music represents a spiritual transformation of the material found earlier in the ardent Love Duet of Act II.

Before beginning your analysis of this passage, play it over or listen to it several times on the CD-ROM, noting the sense of tonal closure between the chords on the downbeats of measures 1 and 11. What compositional device does Wagner use to span the music between the A♭ chords in measures 1 and 7?

_____

_____

Trace the stepwise motion in the vocal line that rises from A♭^{4} to A♭^{5} in measures 1–8. What type of scale does it outline? _____

What enharmonic pivot chord prepares the shift to B major in measures 10–11? _____

This music is filled with analytical problems. For instance, is the opening A♭$^6_4$ an essential tonic chord in second inversion, or is it subordinate to the succeeding E♭ V^7? Play it then express your opinion. _____

_____

Some of the harmonies in this passage may be difficult to classify by Roman numeral symbols.

There are several aspects of this section that relate to certain features of the *Tristan* Prelude, as discussed in Chapter 38 of the text. Can you find a passing allusion to the original Tristan chord notated enharmonically at the same pitch level? _____ Does the opening melodic line (E♭↑A♭–G♮–G♭) remind you of anything similar in the opening of the Prelude? _____

What do you think is the possible tonal origin of the large-scale motion from A♭ to B major? _____

_____

In addition to a harmonic analysis, provide a voice-leading reduction on the staves that follow the score. A space has been provided to append any notes that would serve as further commentary on your analysis.

 Example 38.1

WAGNER: "LIEBESTOD" FROM *TRISTAN UND ISOLDE*, ACT III

Sehr mässig beginnend.

Mild und lei - se wie er lä-chelt, wie das Au - ge
hold er öff - net, seht ihr, Freun-de, säh't ihr's nicht?
Im - mer lich - ter wie _____ er leuch - tet,

Translation: Gently, softly,
how he smiles, how his eyes
he fondly opens!
See you, friends?
See you not?
How he shines
Ever brighter
as the stars shine
high about him.

A.

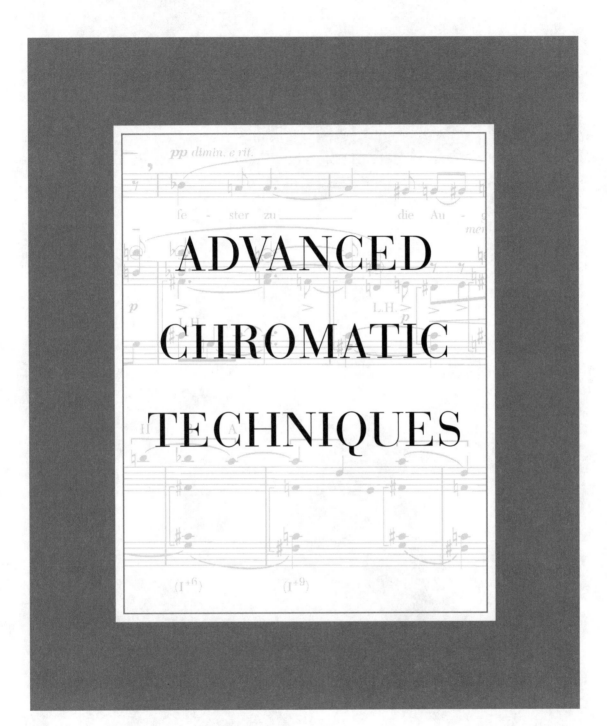

ADVANCED CHROMATIC TECHNIQUES

CHAPTER 39

Chromatic Voice Leading

1 Complete the following chromatic sequences in four-voice texture. Add a functional Roman numeral analysis to the concluding chords of Examples 39.1A and C.

Example 39.1

A.

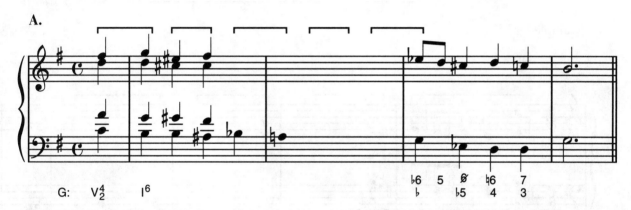

B.

353

C.

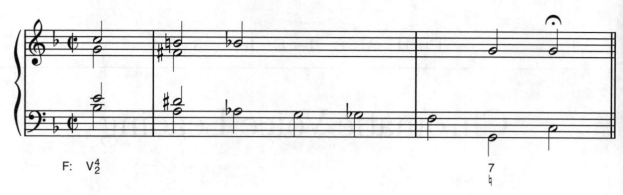

F: V$^4_2$

7♮

2   The following passages contain examples of chromatic parallelism and chromaticism by contrary motion. Continue in strict fashion the sequences that have been started for you. Which chord type is featured in Example 39.2A? _____ Which chord type is featured in Example 39.2B? _____ Which device is exploited in Example 39.2C? _____

Example 39.2

A.

B. (BASED ON CHOPIN'S MAZURKA IN C-SHARP MINOR, OP. 30, NO. 4)

c#: (V)

(iv^6)

C.

3 Realize the figured-bass examples below. Since most of these passages utilize chromatic sequences, provide Roman numerals for only those chords that you feel are the essential harmonies. In examples of prolongation by contrary chromatic motion, denote the harmony that has been prolonged by using a long dash (such as $V^7 \rightarrow V^7$). In the symmetrical chord progression in Example 39.3B, circle the axis chord.

Example 39.3

A.

B.

Bb: (V) ♭7 ♭7 ⌀ 6 7 6 ♯ 7 4 6 ⌀ (V)
     ♭2 ♭   ♯   ♮ ♮ ♯ 2 5 2   ♯
              2   ♯   3

4 Supply an appropriate harmonic analysis for the following passages.

A. How is the dominant prolonged in this excerpt? _____

_____

Example 39.4A

VERDI: QUARTET FROM *RIGOLETTO*, ACT III

B. The two excerpts by Tchaikovsky feature different chromatic techniques. What are the two chord functions that frame Exercise 39.4B, and which chord type does the composer use to bridge these two harmonies? _____ Is the sequence or linear motion strict throughout? _____

Example 39.4B

TCHAIKOVSKY: PIANO CONCERTO NO. 1 IN B-FLAT MINOR, II

F:

C. Make a voice-leading reduction of this interesting passage. Although contrary chromaticism forms its basis, this motion is not strict throughout. Bracket an example of voice exchange and state whether it is diatonic or chromatic. _____

Example 39.4C

TCHAIKOVSKY: WALTZ OF THE FLOWERS FROM *THE NUTCRACKER*, ACT II

D. This ominous music opens the famous Wolf's Glen scene in Weber's *Der Freischütz*. While the passage exhibits a prominent chromatic descent in the bass, it is largely nonsequential. Bracket the small-scale pattern repetition in the middle of the excerpt on the score. Measures 8–10 set up the expectation of tonicizing what key? _____
Why do you think it is not appropriate to assign a Roman numeral function to every chord in this progression? _____

_____

Example 39.4D

WEBER: WOLF'S GLEN SCENE FROM *DER FREISCHÜTZ*, ACT II

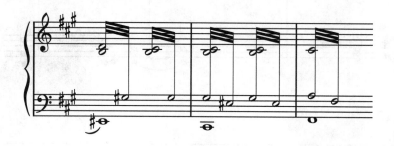

C H A P T E R   4 0

Modulation to Foreign Keys II

1 This pivot-chord example makes use of common diminished sevenths, German augmented sixths, and dominant sevenths. First, spell the original chord in the space provided, then supply the missing Roman numeral or chord symbol in the new foreign key and the new enharmonic spelling. The first example is completed for you.

Example 40.1

D: vii°⁷/V	Bb: V⁷	F: N°⁷/I	a: V⁷/IV
G# B D F	_____	_____	_____
VI : vii°⁷/V	vii : _____	bIII : _____	#iii : _____
E# G# B D			
G : vii°⁷/V	B : Ger $^6_5$	Eb: V⁷/V	C : vii°⁷
_____	_____	_____	_____
bV : _____	bII : _____	#IV : _____	bIII : _____

2 The following five-chord progressions make an enharmonic modulation from the original key to a foreign key. In each case the pivot chord is either a diminished seventh or a German augmented sixth. Analyze each passage with Roman numerals, remembering that the pivot or common chord can be spelled correctly in only one of the two keys.

Example 40.2

A.

A:

B.

D:

C.

Eb:

D.

Bb:

E.

a:

F.

G:

3 Realize the following figured-bass examples. Each example modulates to a foreign key, using either an enharmonic pivot chord or an exact phrase sequence. Your accompanying Roman numeral analysis should indicate how the modulation occurs. In measures 1 and 5 of Example 40.3D, do not begin your four-part texture until beat 2.

Example 40.3

A.

B.

C.

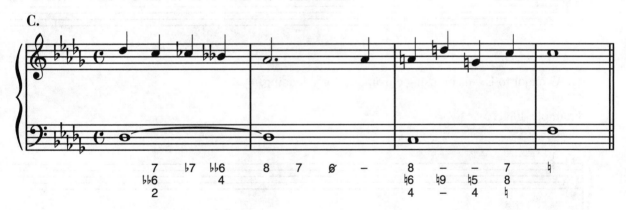

D.

4 Compose three short original passages that modulate to the specified keys utilizing the following methods.

A. D major to F♯ major, using an enharmonic G♯ B D F diminished seventh chord as the pivot.

Example 40.4A

B. F major to E minor, using an enharmonic V⁷-Ger $^6_5$ as the pivot.

Example 40.4B

C. G major to E♭ major, using chromatic voice leading.

Example 40.4C

5 Supply Roman numeral analyses for the following excerpts. Provide voice-leading reductions for Examples 40.5C and F. Be sure to indicate in your analysis how the modulation takes place. Although the first three quotations exhibit tonal shifts by ascending or descending half step, the modulatory technique for each is different.

A. What is the crucial chord that introduces the new key? _____
Which key do you expect it to lead to? _____ Which key does it actually lead to? _____

Example 40.5A

MOZART: SYMPHONY NO. 40 IN G MINOR, K.550, I

B. Which two modulatory procedures link the key of C major at the opening of this passage to the new key of Db major at its conclusion? _____

_____

Example 40.5B

BEETHOVEN: SYMPHONY NO. 1 IN C MAJOR, II

C. In this freely chromatic movement, Haydn has dispensed with the usual key signature and instead has written in all the necessary accidentals. How do you explain the curious notation in measures 5–6? _____

Example 40.5C

HAYDN: STRING QUARTET IN E-FLAT MAJOR, OP. 76, NO. 6, II

D. The opening tonal center of this excerpt is D♭ major. Which chord does it use to modulate back to the original F major tonic? _____ _____ Which other excerpt in Example 40.3 uses a similar harmony?

_____

Example 40.5D

BRAHMS: *EIN DEUTSCHES REQUIEM*, I

E. The following passage forms a transition to the coda, linking VI to V in F minor. There are several transitory tonicizations that occur in rapid succession, including one to a very remote region. Be sure to indicate these in your Roman numeral analysis.

Example 40.5E

CHOPIN: BALLADE IN F MINOR, OP. 52

F. This excerpt opens in F minor. What key is suggested in the last measure? _____ What is its relationship to F minor? _____

_____

Example 40.5F

BACH(?): "HARMONIC LABYRINTH"

G. Where is this passage structurally divided? _____
_____ What tonal relationship exists between the two
separate phrases? _____

Example 40.5G

FRANCK: VIOLIN SONATA IN A MAJOR, I

H. In this developmental passage from the opening movement of Grieg's
Piano Concerto, first determine the framing keys. There are two possible
pivot chords for this modulation—beat 3 of measure 4 or beat 1 of measure
5. Indicate the dual harmonic functions of both these chords.

Example 40.5H

GRIEG: PIANO CONCERTO IN A MINOR, I

C H A P T E R 4 1

Symmetrical Divisions of the Octave

In this chapter we will forgo our usual figured-bass examples and instead concentrate on completing and analyzing various sequences that employ symmetrical root movement by major 2nd, minor 3rd, or major 3rd.

1 In the first three examples, continue the bracketed pattern in exact fashion. Indicate what type of root movement is illustrated in each case. Compare the last chord with the first chord in Example 41.1B; what has happened? _____

In Example 41.1D, continue the omnibus progression by descending minor 3rds begun in the second measure. The half-step motion in the upper parts will switch from voice to voice. Consult Examples 41.10B and 41.12 in the text.

Example 41.1

A.

B.

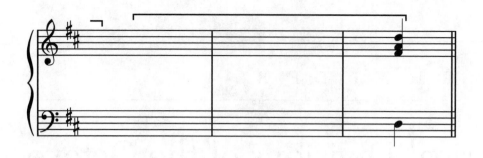

C. (BASED ON CHOPIN'S MAZURKA IN A-FLAT MAJOR, OP. 59, NO. 2)

D.

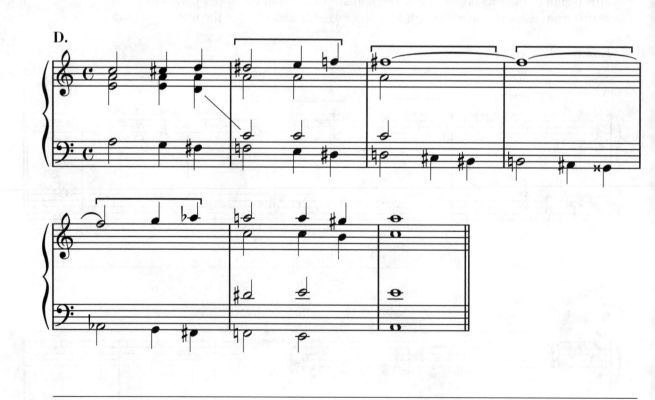

2 The following excerpt is a simplification of a transitional passage from the Scherzo of Beethoven's Symphony No. 9 in D Minor ("Choral"). Chart the successive root movements from measure to measure on the blank staff that is provided. What is the intervallic relationship between the two-measure units? _____ How many of these intervals do we traverse? _____

Example 41.2

BEETHOVEN: SYMPHONY NO. 9 IN D MINOR ("CHORAL"), II

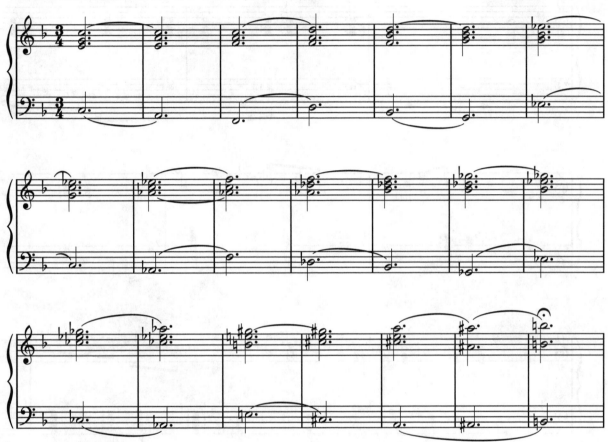

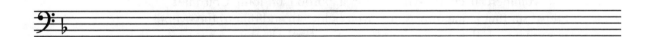

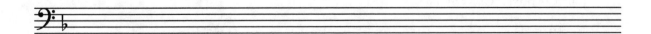

3 Supply appropriate harmonic analyses for the following excerpts, noting the type of sequence and root movement that are used.

A. Which two types of seventh chords are employed in this sequence? _____
_____

Example 41.3A

WAGNER: IMMOLATION SCENE FROM *GÖTTERDÄMMERUNG* (SIMPLIFIED)

B. The commercial chord symbols for a portion of John Coltrane's "Giant Steps" starting in measure 8 are given below. In addition to the overall root movement of this passage, indicate the local diatonic progression that occurs within each two-measure segment.[1]

Example 41.3B

JOHN COLTRANE: "GIANT STEPS"

| E♭MAJ7 | Am7 D7 | GMAJ7 | C♯m7 F♯7 | BMAJ7 | Fm7 B♭7 | E♭MAJ7 |

---

1. According to his daughter, Alice Coltrane, the chords originally played by John Coltrane were E♭MAJ7, Am7, Am9, GMAJ7, C♯m7, C♯m9, BMAJ7, Fm7, Fm9, and E♭MAJ7.

C. This excerpt provides a modulatory link to the following waltz in B♭ major. What type of sequence occurs in measures 2–7? _____

_____

Example 41.3C

TCHAIKOVSKY: *SLEEPING BEAUTY*, ACT I

D. This strange passage was actually composed during the Baroque period. Chart the sequential root movement in the empty staff provided. How is this excerpt similar to the Beethoven excerpt in Example 41.2? _____

_____

What is remarkable about the partwriting connections between consecutive chords? _____

_____

Example 41.3D

DOMENICO SCARLATTI: SONATA IN E MINOR, K. 394

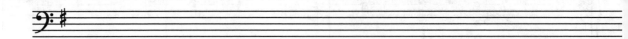

E. How would you justify the statement that this passage from Chopin's D-flat Major Nocturne represents a dominant prolongation? _____

_____

Note the common tone (F♯ = G♭) in the upper voices.

Example 41.3E

CHOPIN: NOCTURNE IN D-FLAT MAJOR, OP. 27, NO. 2 (REDUCTION OF MM. 40–46)

F. Here the rising chromaticism occurs in the bass voice; compare with Example 41.3B. What two keys does this passage link? _____
In the upper voices, what do you observe about the voice leading in the chord connections of this chromatic progression? _____
_____

Using the empty staff, rewrite these parts, using octave displacement to produce more standard partwriting.

Example 41.3F

BEETHOVEN: STRING QUARTET IN B-FLAT MAJOR, OP. 18, NO. 6

G. This excerpt contains a number of different exotic chords and compositional devices. List some of its unusual features, citing measure numbers.

_____

Except for the last key, the tonics may be implied.

Example 41.3G

FRANCK: SYMPHONY IN D MINOR, III

H. Finally, this transcendental passage from the "Good Friday Music" of *Parsifal* contains an interesting mixture of chromatic and diatonic techniques. After plotting its harmonic origin and goal, see if you can find a dividing point near the middle of the progression that mimics the final cadential approach.

Example 41.3H

WAGNER: "GOOD FRIDAY MUSIC" FROM *PARSIFAL*, ACT III

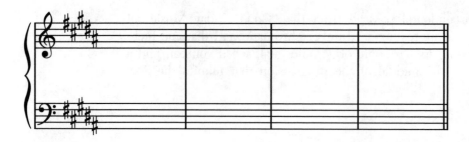

4 Compose an original passage for piano, using a harmonic progression that divides the octave symmetrically. Try to link the bass root movement with additional chords, as in the passages given in Example 41.1.

Example 41.4

APPENDIX 3

An Introduction to
Species Counterpoint

1 The examples below provide a choice of cantus firmi to use in your counterpoint exercises from first to fifth species. They may appear as either the top or
bottom voice in two-voice texture; if you wish to employ them as the lower
part, move them down an octave and write them in the bass clef.

Example A3.1

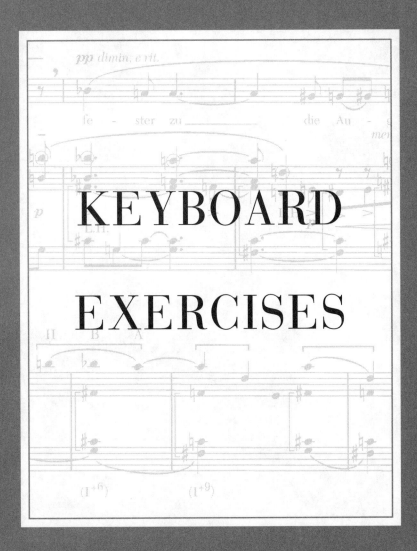

KEYBOARD

EXERCISES

Keyboard Exercises for Chapter 1

1 Play the indicated pitches in both treble and bass clefs and identify their proper octave designation ($F\sharp^4$, C^2, $E\flat^3$, etc.).

Example K1.1

2 Play any simple diatonic interval that your instructor indicates above or below the indicated pitches. Exercise K1.2 provides some practice examples.

Example K1.2

P5   M3   M2   m3   m7   M6   m2   m6   P4   M7

3 Analyze the bracketed successions of intervals. You may wish to write the names of the intervals into the music. Then continue these intervallic patterns in strict fashion until you reach the final tone that is given. Do not write in the names of the notes of the pattern you are continuing.

Example K1.3

A.

B.

C.

D.

4 Play the indicated augmented or diminished intervals using each pitch given below. Build the interval upward or downward as indicated by the arrow. Identify the name of the pitch you are playing.

A. Augmented prime, augmented 5th, augmented 2nd, augmented 4th, augmented 6th.

Example K1.4A

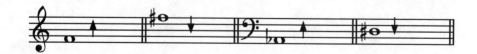

B. Diminished octave, diminished 4th, diminished 7th, diminished 5th.

Example K1.4B

Keyboard Exercises for Chapter 3

For the examples in this chapter, use major and minor keys having up to four sharps or flats.

1 Play the major scale and the three forms of the minor scale (natural, melodic, and harmonic) in all keys having up to four sharps or flats. Recite the interval between successive scale degrees as you play (major 2nd, minor 2nd, augmented 2nd, etc.). Give the proper key signature for each scale.

2 Choose a key and play (1) its relative major or melodic minor scale and (2) its parallel major or melodic minor scale. Then repeat this procedure for five other keys of your choice.

3 Play the indicated scale degrees in keys that your instructor gives you:

A. Major: $\hat{1}$ $\hat{6}$ $\hat{3}$ $\hat{5}$ $\hat{7}$ $\hat{4}$ $\hat{2}$ $\hat{3}$ $\hat{6}$ $\hat{4}$ $\hat{7}$ $\hat{2}$ $\hat{5}$ $\hat{1}$

B. Minor: $\hat{1}$ $\hat{4}$ $\flat\hat{6}$ $\hat{2}$ $\sharp\hat{7}$ $(\flat)\hat{3}$ $\sharp\hat{6}$ $\hat{4}$ $\hat{5}$ $\flat\hat{7}$ $\hat{2}$ $\flat\hat{3}$ $\hat{1}$ $\hat{5}$

4 Using the seven-note rhythmic pattern $\frac{4}{4}$ ♩ ♩ ♩ ♩ | ♩ ♩ ♩ ‖ , improvise melodic phrases in major and minor keys up to three sharps or flats. Each phrase should begin on either $\hat{1}$, $\hat{3}$, or $\hat{5}$ and end with one of the standard melodic cadences, either conclusive or inconclusive.

Keyboard Exercises for Chapter 4

1 Continue the following pattern of major triads (up a perfect 5th, down a perfect 4th) until you reach an F♯ root-position triad. Then reverse the direction, starting from a C^4 triad (up a perfect 4th, down a perfect 5th), to cover the flat accidentals. First practice the major-chord succession as shown below, then alter it to a minor-chord succession. You may use one hand only or double in octaves, using both hands.

Example K4.1

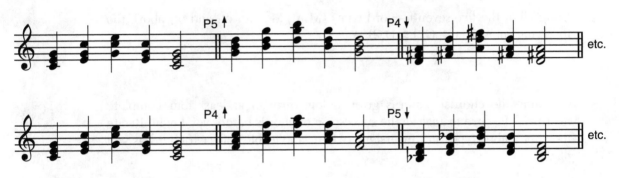

2 Play first-inversion augmented (+) or diminished (o) triads as indicated, using each of the pitches given below as the chordal 3rd of the triad. The first example will serve as a model.

Example K4.2

3 Using your right hand, play the triad above the given notes as indicated by the figured-bass symbols (see the first model). Observe the different key signatures in each example.

Example K4.3

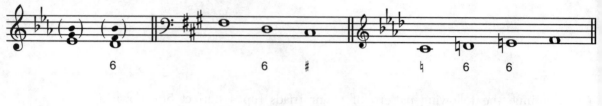

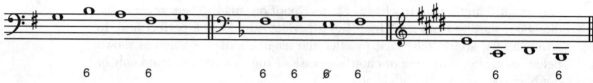

4 Build all of the five seventh-chord types (Mm^7, M^7, m^7, ø^7, and o^7) above the following notes: E, C♯, G, F♯, D, B, A.

5 Continue the chordal patterns given below through at least four complete measures. Be sure to analyze the succession of chords before you begin. Recite the root, chord type, and inversions (where applicable) of each chord as you play it.

Example K4.5

Keyboard Exercises for
Chapter 5

In the following examples, realize the figured bass in four-voice texture; employ only close and occasionally neutral or open/octave structure in which the soprano and tenor lie exactly an octave apart. Play the upper three voices with your right hand and the bass with your left hand.

1 Continue Examples K5.1A and B through the circle of 5ths for at least eight major keys, using the illustrations below as models. Then change the chords to minor triads and repeat the patterns. Repeat these procedures in Example K5.1C, which employs both open/octave and close structure.

Example K5.1

C.

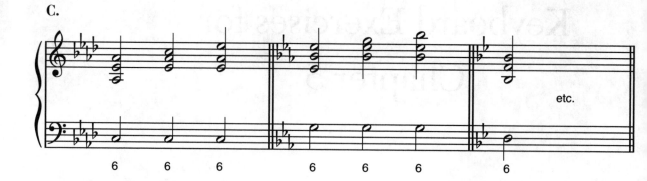

etc.

2 Play the triads indicated by the figured-bass symbols in four-voice texture, using either close or open/octave structure for the first inversions. Recite the root, inversion, and chord type of each sonority.

Example K5.2

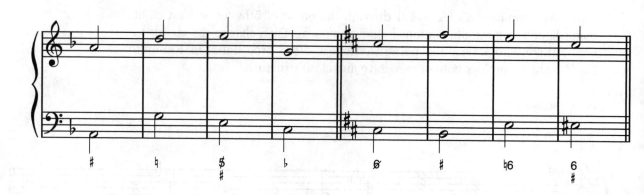

3 Realize the figured-bass examples given below by filling in the alto and tenor voices. Do not write the notes in the music. Excerpt for the triad marked O/O, play all the chords in close structure. Be sure to observe both the figured bass symbol and the key signature.

Example K5.3

A.   **B.**

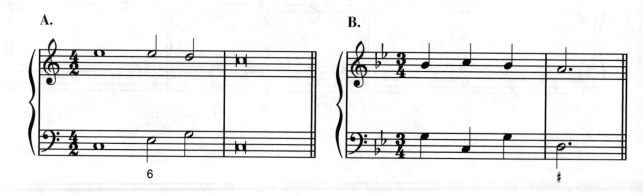

C.

D.

O/O

E.

F.

Keyboard Exercises for
Chapter 9

1 **A.** The following harmonic models are based on progressions found in typical authentic cadences. First play them as written in both the major and minor mode, then transpose them to all keys with signatures of three or more sharps or flats. Do not change the partwriting connections between chords during your transpositions.

Example K9.1A

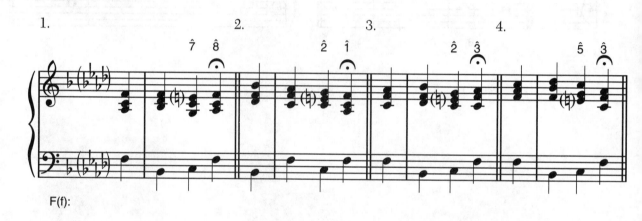

B. The following harmonic models are based on progressions found in typical half cadences. Play them in the manner prescribed above in Example K9.1A.

Example K9.1B

2 Using only close structure, realize the figured bass in the following phrases. Identify the Roman numeral function of each chord. Watch for raised 3rds (♯ or ♮) in the exercises.

Example K9.2

A.

B.

C.

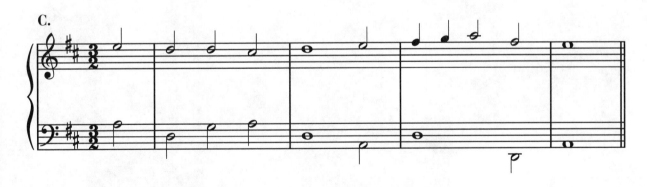

D.

3 Improvise six seven-note melodic phrases, ending each with a two-chord harmonic cadential formula. Use different soprano scale degrees in your cadence. You may choose any major or minor keys. The two models serve as examples.

Example K9.3

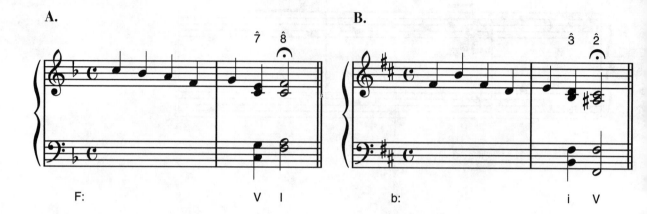

Keyboard Exercises for Chapter 10

1 Play each of the following progressions in both C major and C minor then transpose them to four other major and minor keys. The key signatures and accidentals in parentheses in this and similar models in later chapters always represent both C major and C minor. Observe the approach to and resolution of the chordal 7th in each example. In three of these exercises the chordal 5th of the V⁷ has been omitted and the root doubled for smoother partwriting.

Example K10.1

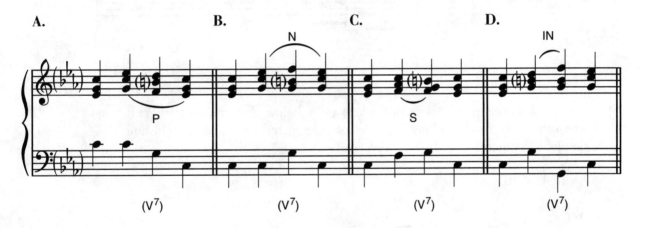

2 Realize the following figured-bass examples, using close structure for all chords. Make sure that your chord spelling agrees with the figured bass. Explain the treatment of the chordal 7th in each V⁷ that you play. All circled notes are dissonant embellishing tones.

Example K10.2

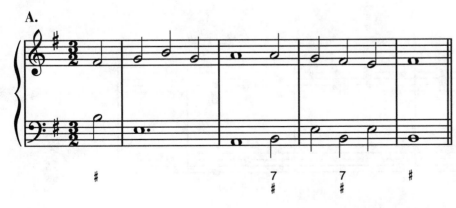

B.

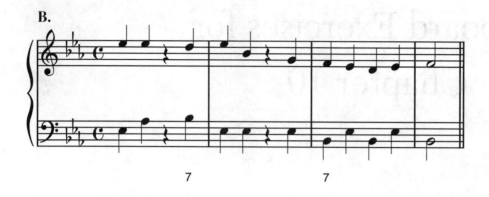

C.

3 Play the following progressions in the keys given below, then transpose them to four other keys. Point out any examples of arpeggiated tonic and embellishing dominant harmonies.

Example K10.3

A.

B.

4 Harmonize the following two phrases in four-voice texture, using only I, IV, V, and V^7 chords in root position in major and minor keys. Use a V^7 to support each note marked with an arrow. Make sure that the chordal 7th is approached and resolved correctly.

Example K10.4

A.

E:

B.

g:

Keyboard Exercises for Chapter 11

1 Play the following progressions then transpose them to major and minor keys of at least three sharps or flats. In most cases the I⁶ and IV⁶ chords must be played in open/octave position, with an octave and a 5th or 4th in the right hand. Close structure is assumed for the remaining harmonies.

Example K11.1

A.

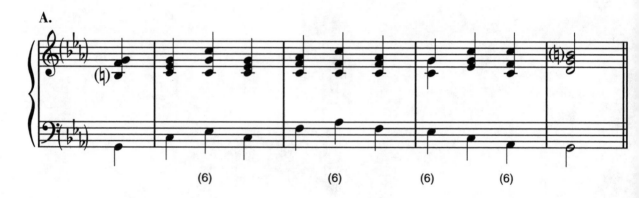

B.

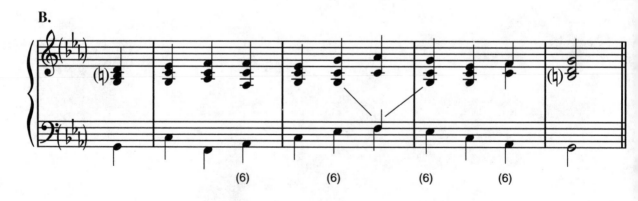

2 Realize the following figured-bass examples in four-voice texture, using the structures recommended for first inversions and root-position chords in Example K11.1. Provide each exercise with appropriate Roman numerals.

Example K11.2

A.

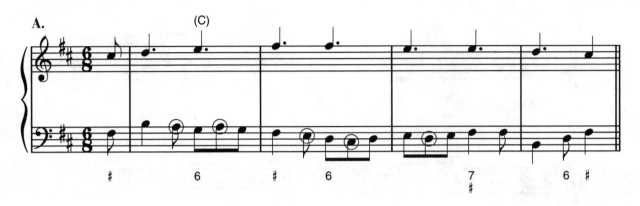

B.

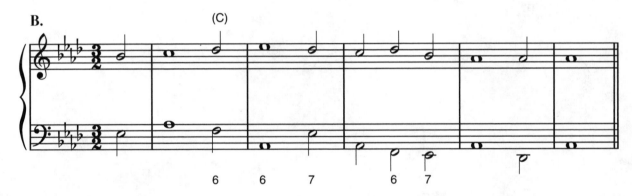

C.

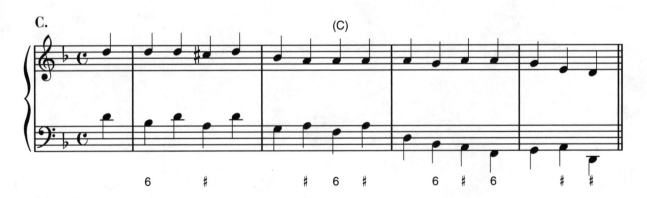

3 Harmonize the two phrases below. Use a first-inversion I or IV for those notes marked with an arrow. Use your inversions to produce a better melodic line in the bass voice.

Example K11.3

A.

A:

B.

f#:

Keyboard Exercises for
Chapter 13

1 Play the three-chord models below in major and minor keys having up to four sharps or flats. Explain how the 7th is treated in each case.

Example K13.1

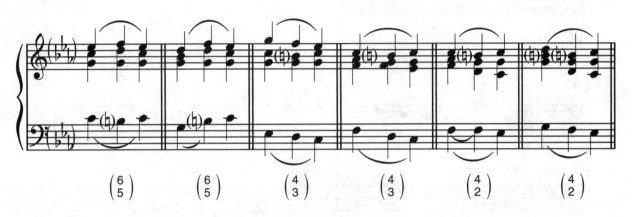

$$\begin{pmatrix} 6 \\ 5 \end{pmatrix} \qquad \begin{pmatrix} 6 \\ 5 \end{pmatrix} \qquad \begin{pmatrix} 4 \\ 3 \end{pmatrix} \qquad \begin{pmatrix} 4 \\ 3 \end{pmatrix} \qquad \begin{pmatrix} 4 \\ 2 \end{pmatrix} \qquad \begin{pmatrix} 4 \\ 2 \end{pmatrix}$$

2 In addition to inversions of the V^7, the following progressions contain typical uses of the V^6 and vii^{o6} embellishing chords. Play each example, then transpose it to keys having at least three sharps or flats in each mode. Provide a Roman numeral analysis of each passage.

Example K13.2

A.

B.

3 Realize the following figured-bass examples, using four-voice texture and primarily close structure; for those chords marked with arrows, use open/octave spacing. All embellishing tones are circles. Example K13.3C contains a prolongation of the dominant seventh chord.

Example K13.3

C.

D.

4 Harmonize the following tunes in four-voice settings, using the harmonies available to us through Chapter 13. Strive for smooth voice leading in your bass lines; the use of embellishing dominants should aid in the generation of better melodic lines for the bass.

Example K13.4

A.

B.

Keyboard Exercises for
Chapter 14

1 The four cadential formulas below incorporate various uses of the supertonic triad or seventh chord. Play the formulas then transpose them to keys of up to three sharps or flats; observe the melodic scale degrees in the soprano. Improvise a short melodic segment of three notes to lead into each cadence thus producing a complete phrase.

Example K14.1

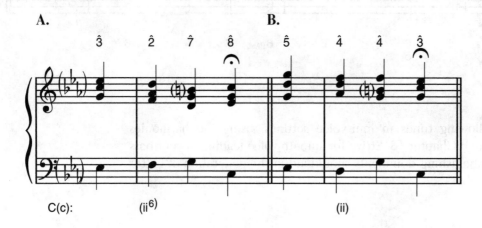

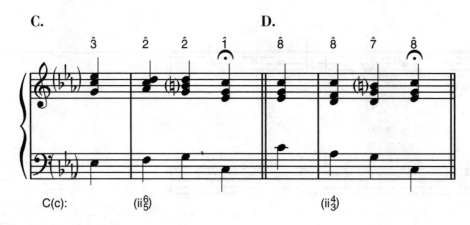

2 The following progressions represent various ways of embellishing the tonic using pre-dominant harmonies within the phrase. Transpose each to three other keys, major and minor.

Example K14.2

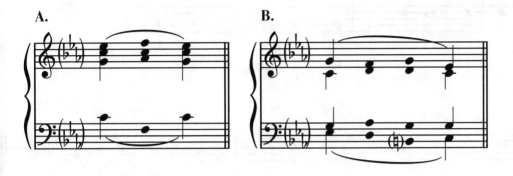

3 Realize the following figured-bass examples and identify all examples of supertonic triads or seventh chords. Remember that in the IV⁶ or ii⁶ triads, either close or open/octave structure is possible. In close structure you may double the soprano or an occasional inner voice at the unison. Why do you think it is necessary to double the third in the second chord of Example K14.3C?

Example K14.3

4 Harmonize the following hymn phrases using appropriate pre-dominant chords in both cadential and embellishing roles. Name two ways of approaching the first cadence in "St. Fulbert."

Example K14.4

A. "St. Michael"

B. "St. Fulbert"

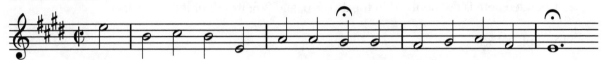

Keyboard Exercises for
Chapter 15

1   The following progressions feature typical suspensions. Transpose them to major and minor keys with up to three sharps or flats. Notice that the suspended note is *not* doubled in the 4-3, 7-6, and 2-3; it *is* doubled in the 9-8.

Example K15.1

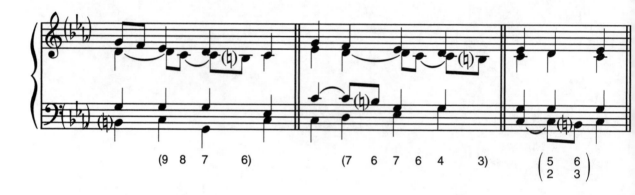

2   Play the following chains of suspensions then transpose them to three other keys, both major and minor. Example K15.2B employs only three voices; why are the suspensions necessary here? Identify each type of suspension as you play it.

Example K15.2

A.

B.

3 Realize the following figured-bass examples, employing close or open/octave structure. Be sure that you correctly prepare and resolve all suspensions. Locate any examples of a change of bass and an ornamental suspension.

Example K15.3

A.

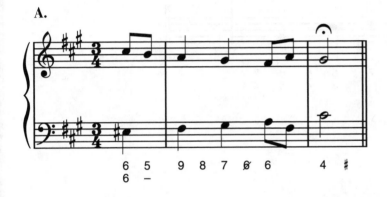

B.

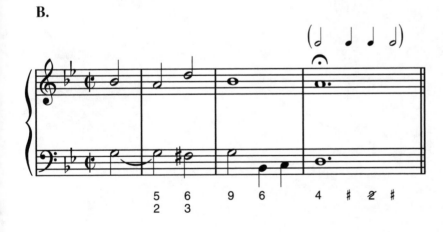

C.

6 5   7 6 7 6   4 3 8 7   4 3
6 –

D.

(C)

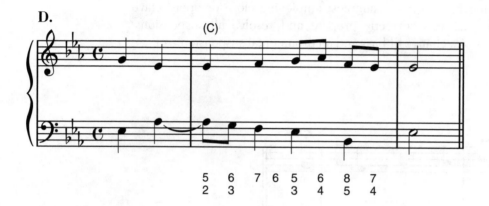

5   6   7 6 5   6   8   7
2   3   3   4   5   4

Keyboard Exercises for Chapter 16

1 The following progressions employ cadential $^6_4$ chords. In each case, the mode (M or m), Roman numerals, and soprano scale degrees are provided. Fill in the remaining notes to make a four-voice texture. Play each progression in three different keys of your choice.

Example K16.1

A. $\hat{5}$ $\hat{4}$ $\hat{3}$ $\hat{2}$ $\hat{1}$ **B.** $\hat{3}$ $\hat{2}$ $\hat{8}$ $\sharp\hat{7}$ $\hat{8}$ **C.** $\hat{5}$ $\hat{5}$ $\hat{5}$ $\hat{4}$ $\hat{3}$ $\hat{2}$

(M) I⁶ IV $\begin{smallmatrix}6&5\\4&3\end{smallmatrix}$ V I   (m) i⁶ ii°⁶ $\begin{smallmatrix}6&5\\4&3\end{smallmatrix}$ V i   (M) I V I⁶ IV $\begin{smallmatrix}6&5\\4&3\end{smallmatrix}$ V

2 Passing and neighboring $^6_4$ chords occur in the following three models. Play each one then transpose it to the keys of A, G, and F major and their parallel minors.

Example K16.2

A.

B.

C.

3 Realize the following figured-bass examples. Indicate as you play all occurrences of $^6_4$'s and any other linear chords that we have studied.

Example K16.3

A.

B.

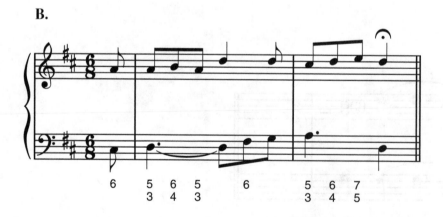

C.

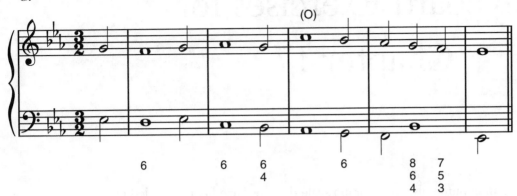

4 Harmonize the following tune in four-voice texture. Play an appropriate $\frac{6}{4}$ chord to support each note marked with an arrow. The labels above the brackets denote the manner in which the dissonant 4th, which may or may not be the melodic note, is approached and resolved.

Example K16.4

Keyboard Exercises for
Chapter 17

1 The mode, Roman numerals, and soprano scale degrees have been provided in Example K17.1. Play the resulting progressions in four-voice texture in three keys of your choice. Avoid parallels in the deceptive cadence in Example K17.1C.

Example K17.1

A. $\hat{3}$ $\hat{3}$ $\hat{2}$ $\hat{2}$ $\hat{1}$ **B.** $\hat{8}$ $\hat{7}$ $\hat{6}$ $\hat{5}$ $\hat{3}$ **C.** $\hat{8}$ $\hat{8}$ $\hat{8}$ $\hat{7}$ $\hat{8}$ **D.** $\hat{1}$ $\hat{2}$ $\hat{3}$ $\hat{4}$ $\hat{5}$

(m) i VI ii° V i   (M) I iii IV V I   (M) I IV I⁶ V vi   (m) i VII III iv⁶ V

2 Play each progression then transpose it a major 2nd higher and a major 2nd lower; use both major and minor modes in Example K17.2A.

Example K17.2

A.

B.
(major only)

C.
(minor only)

3 Realize the following figured-bass examples and provide appropriate Roman numerals.

Example K17.3

A.

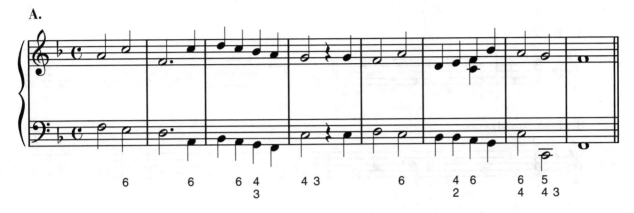

B.

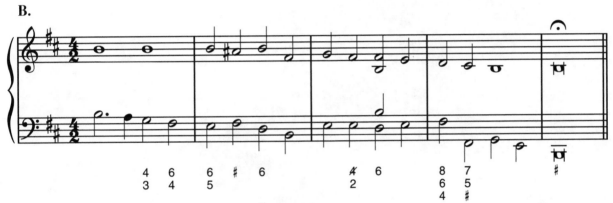

C.

4 Harmonize the following two melodies using appropriate mediant and sub-mediant chords. For one of them, use a texture other than four-voice chorale style.

Example K17.4

A. "Irish"

B. "Lobe den Herren"

Keyboard Exercises for Chapter 19

1 The following chord progressions use leading-tone seventh chords; Roman numerals and soprano scale degrees are provided. Play these progressions in minor keys having up to four sharps or flats.

Example K19.1

A. $\hat{3}$ $\hat{4}$ $\hat{3}$ **B.** $\hat{8}$ $\hat{7}$ $\hat{8}$ **C.** $\hat{3}$ $\hat{4}$ $\hat{2}$ $\hat{5}$ **D.** $\hat{1}$ $\hat{2}$ $\hat{3}$ $\hat{2}$

   i   vii°7   i   i   vii°$^6_5$ i^6 i   iv   vii°$^4_3$ i^6 i   vii°$^4_2$ $^6_4$ $^5_\sharp$

                                                              V

2 Continue the harmonic sequence below, concluding with the key of **F♯** minor. Transpose to another octave whenever necessary. Identify the various inversions of the leading-tone seventh chords.

Example K19.2

3 The following short progressions feature typical uses of the tonic and subdominant seventh chords. Play the progressions then transpose them to five other keys of your choice.

Example K19.3

(IV⁷) → (IV^7)

A. B. C.

(IV^7) (IV^6_5) $(I^7 \; IV^7)$

4 Realize the following figured-bass examples and analyze them with Roman numerals. Be wary of the opening progression in Example K19.4C, as it may contain parallels.

Example K19.4

A.

$$\begin{array}{cccccccc} 6 & 7 & \emptyset & 7 & 9 & 8 & & 7 & 6 & 4 & & 6 & - \\ & 5 & - & & & & & 4 & 3 & 4 & & 4 & 3 \\ & & & & & & & 2 & & & & & \end{array}$$

B.

$$\begin{array}{ccccccccc} 4 & 7 & & & 4 & 6 & 6 & 7 & 6 & & \# & - \\ 2 & & & & 3 & & & & 5 & & \end{array}$$

C.

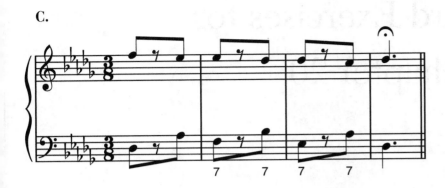

5 Make a four-voice setting of the following tunes. Use leading-tone sevenths to support those melodic notes marked with arrows. In addition, find appropriate places for tonic and subdominant sevenths.

Example K19.5

Keyboard Exercises for
Chapter 20

1   Given modes, Roman numerals, and soprano scale degrees, play the two cycle-of-fifths progressions below, using the keys of D, F, and A♭ major for the first and the keys of E, G, and B minor for the second. Example K20.1A uses root position triads exclusively; Example K20.1B alternates root position with first inversion.

Example K20.1

A. $\hat{5}$ $\hat{6}$ $\hat{4}$ $\hat{5}$ $\hat{3}$ $\hat{4}$ $\hat{2}$ $\hat{3}$

(M)   I   IV   vii°   iii   vi   ii   V   I

B. $\hat{3}$ $\hat{4}$ $\hat{2}$ $\hat{3}$ $\hat{1}$ $\hat{2}$ $\sharp\hat{7}$ $\hat{1}$

(m)   i   iv⁶   VII   III⁶   VI   ii°⁶   V   i

2   Continue the following diatonic sequences in strict fashion to the end of each passage. Then transpose each one to another key of your choice.

Example K20.2

A.

B.

C.

D.

(7 6̸)

3 Realize the following figured-bass examples. Identify the type of sequential root movement used in each passage.

Example K20.3

A.

6   6   6   6 7 8 7   6

B.

4   Harmonize the tunes below in four-voice texture using the appropriate sequential progressions implied by the melodies.

Example K20.4

A. SWEDISH FOLK SONG

B. "ST. DENIS"

Keyboard Exercises for
Chapter 21

1 In the following harmonic sequences, the successive scale degrees of the major and minor mode are preceded by secondary dominants—V^7's in Example 1A and $°7$'s in Example 1B. Play these sequences then transpose them to two other keys of your choice. Identify the function of each chord as you play.

Example K21.1

2 Continue the sequence of applied dominant seventh chords in the two following progressions. Then transpose each to one other key of your choice. Recite the chord functions as you play.

Example K21.2

A.

a:

B.

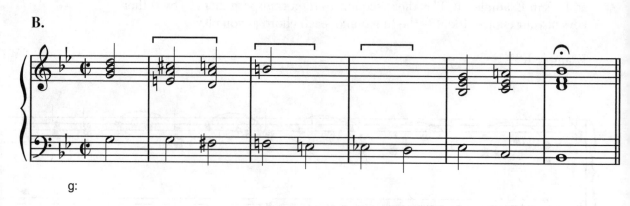

g:

3 Realize the following figured-bass examples in four-voice texture, naming each secondary dominant as you play it.

Example K21.3

A.

B.

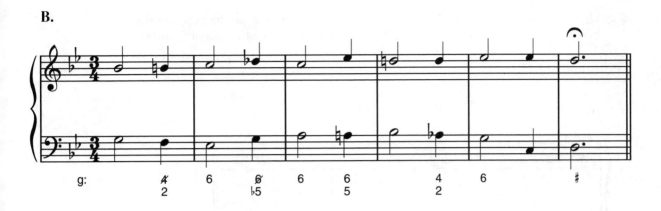

C.

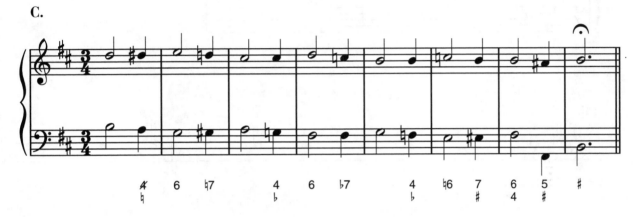

D.

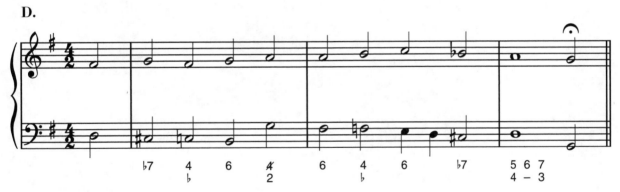

4 Harmonize the following two phrases, using applied chords to support the notes marked with arrows. Exercise K21.4A may be set in either E♭ or C minor.

Example K21.4

A.

E♭:

B.

D:

Keyboard Exercises for
Chapter 22

1 The following phrases make a common-chord modulation to either the dominant key ($\boxed{V}$) from major or the relative major key ($\boxed{III}$) from minor. Harmonize the phrases in four-voice texture, making an appropriate cadence in the new key. Use the first chord in each bracket as your pivot.

Example K22.1

2 Realize the following figured-bass examples, all of which feature modulations to the dominant or relative minor. Some remain in the new key; others conclude in the original tonal center. State where the pivot chord occurs. Do any employ chromatic modulation?

Example K22.2

A.

3 Play three separate modulations from a major key to its dominant ($\boxed{\text{V}}$) in four-voice texture, using a different pivot chord in each passage. Then do the same thing from a minor key to its relative major key ($\boxed{\text{III}}$), again using a different pivot for each modulation. Employ a minimum of five to seven chords. Create a smooth, basically stepwise soprano line that leads to an authentic cadence in the new key.

Keyboard Exercises for
Chapter 23

1   Given the mode, Roman numerals, and soprano scale degrees, play the following cycle-of-fifths progressions; then transpose the first to the keys of D, B♭, and A major and the second to the keys of E, G, and F♯ minor. In Example K23.1A, why is it necessary that you alternate complete with incomplete seventh chords?

Example K23.1

A. $\hat{5}$ $\hat{6}$ $\hat{6}$ $\hat{5}$ $\hat{5}$ $\hat{4}$ $\hat{4}$ $\hat{3}$

(M)   I   IV⁷   vii°⁷   iii⁷   vi⁷   ii⁷   V⁷   I

B. $\hat{3}$ $\hat{3}$ $\hat{2}$ $\hat{2}$ $\hat{1}$ $\hat{1}$ $\#\hat{7}$ $\hat{1}$

(m)   i   iv⁶₅   VII   III⁶₅   VI   ii°⁶₅   V   i

2   Continue the following diatonic sequences to the end of each passage. Then transpose them to one other key of your choice. Identify the underlying root movement for each progression.

Example K23.2

A.

B.

3 Realize the following figured-bass examples in four-voice texture.

Example K23.3

A.

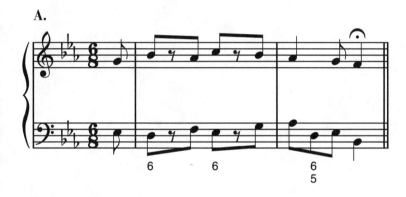

B.

C.

4 Make a four-voice setting of this melody using a cycle of fifth-related seventh chords.

Example K23.4

f#:

Keyboard Exercises for Chapter 27

1. Realize the following figured-bass examples. Which scale degree is tonicized at each cadence? Are these notes closely related to each other and the original tonic key? Recite the chord functions as you play each passage and identify the means of modulation.

Example K27.1

A.

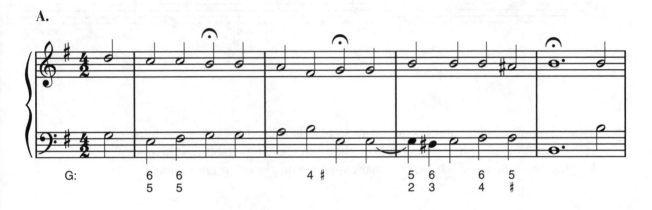

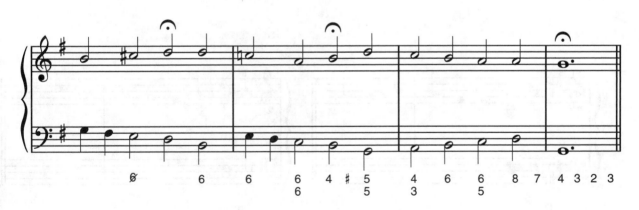

B.

2. The following melodic phrases modulate to closely related keys. Make a four-voice setting of each phrase, making sure that your cadence establishes the new key; the notes indicated with arrows mark appropriate places for pivot chords.

Example K27.2

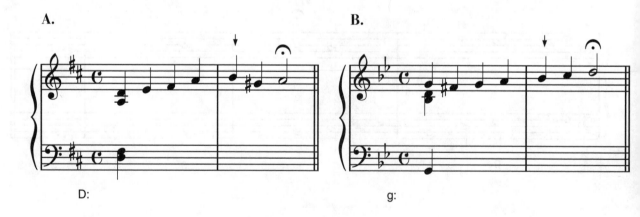

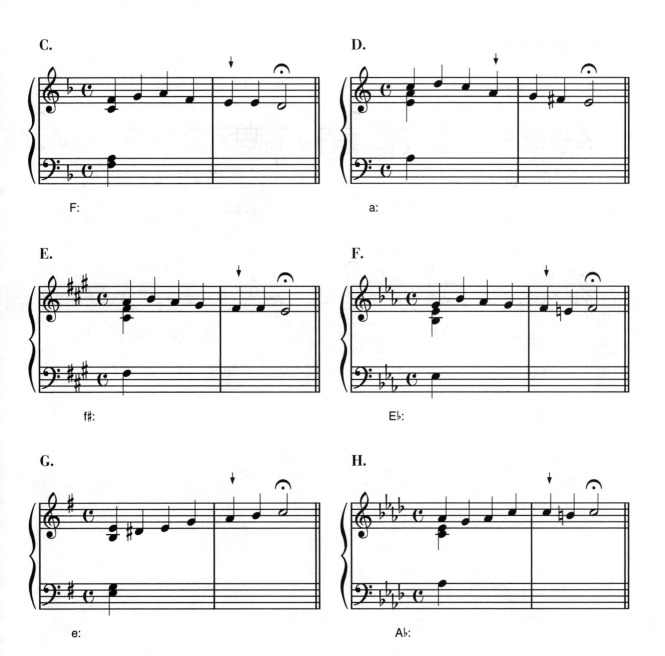

3 The following melodic phrases make use of chromatic inflection to modulate to closely related keys. Again, make a four-voice setting with your cadence in the new key. The note on which the chromatic inflection occurs is denoted with an arrow. Your tonal goal is indicated at the beginning of each phrase.

Example K27.3

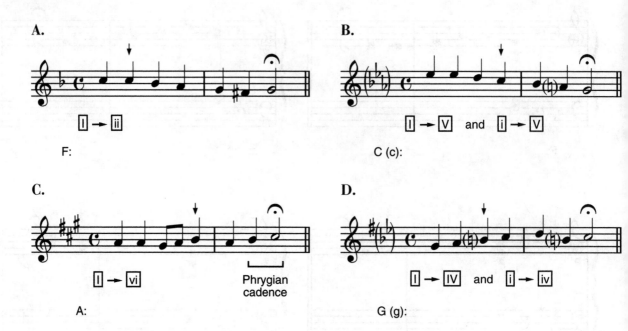

Keyboard Exercises for
Chapter 28

1 Play the root position of the following mixture chords—iv, ii°⁷, ♭VI, ♭III, and III—in the following major keys: D, F, A, G, and B♭. Use four-voice texture.

2 Play the following voice-leading models then transpose them to the keys indicated below. Identify each mixture chord as you perform it.

A. Transpose to C major and A major.

Example K28.2A

B. Transpose to B♭ major and C major.

Example K28.2B

C. Transpose to A major and E♭ major. This passage contains several chord progressions that are typical of rock. What type of root movement is employed in the last two measures?

Example K28.2C

3 Using four-voice texture, play the following progressions in the keys of D, E♭, A, and B♭ major. Roman numerals and soprano scale degrees have been provided for you.

Example K28.3

A. $\hat{5}$ $\hat{4}$ $\hat{4}$ $\hat{3}$ $\hat{3}$ $\hat{4}$ $\hat{2}$ $\hat{3}$ **B.** $\hat{3}$ $\hat{2}$ $\hat{2}$ $\hat{1}$ $\hat{1}$ $\hat{1}$
   I   ii$^{ø4}_{2}$ V$^{6}_{5}$ I   vi   IV   ii$^{ø6}_{5}$ I   I   ii$^{ø6}_{5}$ V   ♭VI   iv   I

4 Realize the following figured-bass examples and identify the mixture chords in each passage.

Example K28.4

A.

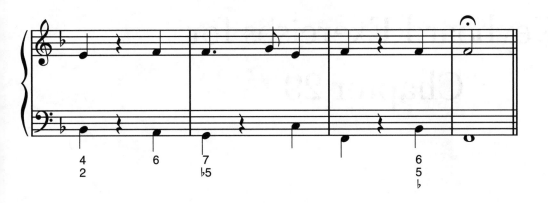

B.

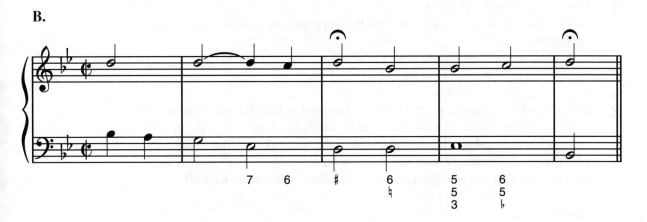

Keyboard Exercises for Chapter 29

1 Play the four-voice progression ♭II⁶–V–I in the keys of D, B, C, A, and G minor. Keep scale degrees ♭$\hat{2}$ or $\hat{4}$ in the soprano; avoid doubling the altered supertonic.

2 The following passages, most of whose bass notes lack figured-bass symbols, contain various treatments of Neapolitan harmony. Scan the outer voices to determine the implied chords then realize the examples in four-voice texture. Identify the Neapolitan chord functions as you play them. Some examples may contain modulations; watch for potential parallels in Example K29.2B.

Example K29.2

B.

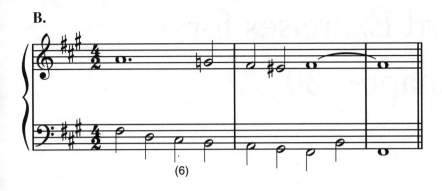

3 Given the keys and soprano lines, fill in the following cadential formulas, using a ♭II⁶ on those notes marked with arrows. Create two different settings for Example K29.3A.

Example K29.3

A.   **B.**

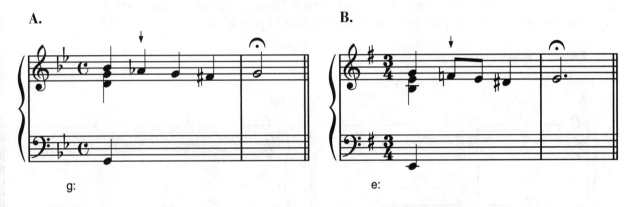

g: e:

C.

f:

4 Harmonize the following melody, using two examples of Neapolitan harmony.

Example K29.4

Keyboard Exercises for
Chapter 30

1 Play an It⁶, Fr⁴₃, and Ger⁶₅ in keys having up to three sharps or flats. Use four-voice texture and resolve the augmented sixth chord to dominant harmony or, in the case of the Ger⁶₅, to a ⁶₄.

2 Play the following cadential progressions, which feature various augmented sixth chords. Then transpose them to two other keys of your choice.

Example K30.2

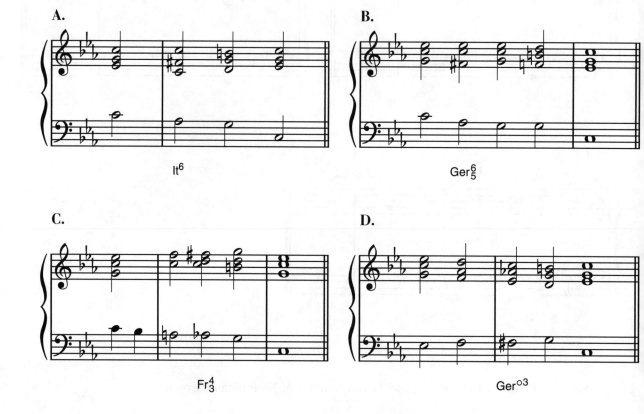

3   Complete the following sequence of secondary Italian sixth chords.

Example K30.3

4   Realize the following figured-bass examples, naming the augmented sixth chords as you play them. Watch for possible key changes.

Example K30.4

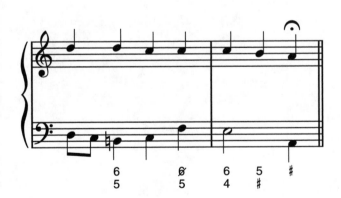

5 Make a four-voice setting of the following melody, using at least two examples of augmented sixth chords.

Example K30.5

Keyboard Exercises for
Chapter 32

1 Play the following passage then transpose it to two other keys of your choice. Cite all examples of augmented triads as you play them and identify their linear function.

Example K32.1

2 The following progressions contain examples of altered dominant sevenths, common-tone diminished sevenths, and augmented sixths. Play each progression in major keys having up to three sharps or flats.

Example K32.2

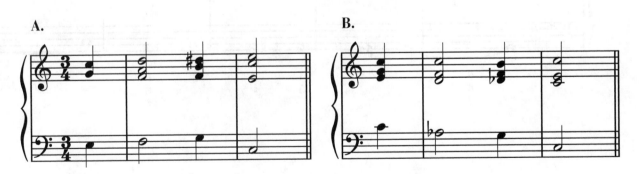

C.

D.

3   Realize the following figured-bass examples in four voices and identify any examples of embellishing chromatic chords as you play them. These examples are more demanding than those in previous chapters; prepare them carefully.

Example K32.3

A.

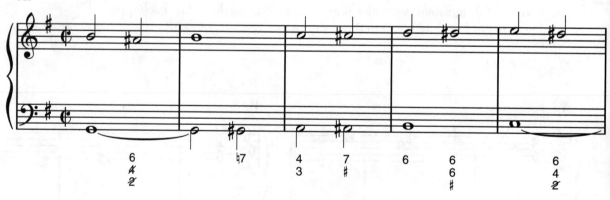

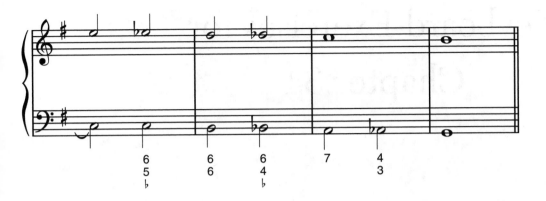

4   Harmonize the following two short phrases using appropriate embellishing chromatic chords.

Example K32.4

Keyboard Exercises for
Chapter 34

1 Realize the following figured-bass passages. Identify the foreign key relationship and pivot chord in any modulation that moves away from and back to the original key center. Because of the foreign key changes, the figured-bass symbols contain a high number of altered intervals, so proceed slowly. Remember that the numbers always refer to the intervals above the bass note in terms of the given key signature, not the key at the moment.

Example K34.1

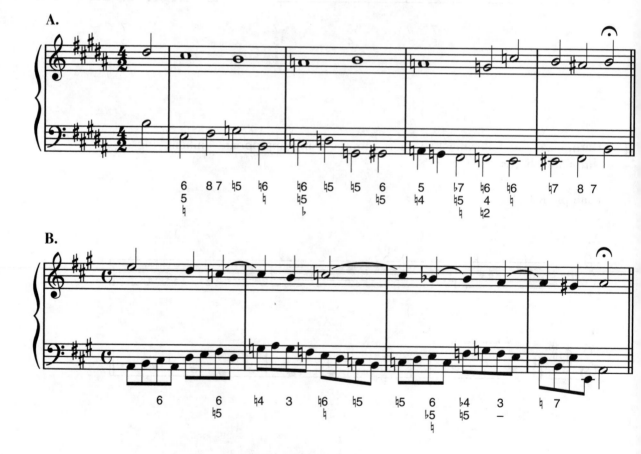

2 The following short melodic phrases modulate to various foreign keys. In addition to the new key, the pivot chord and soprano line are provided. Fill in the other voices to complete the progression, making sure that you end with an appropriate cadence in the new key.

Example K34.2

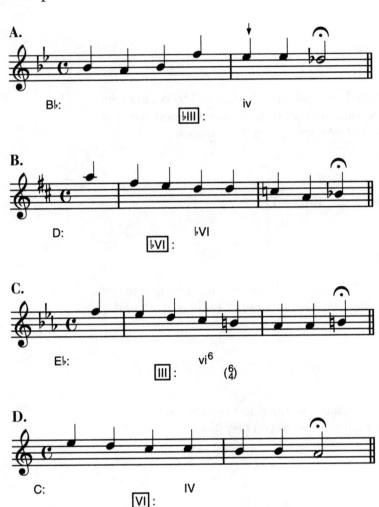

3 Choosing any major key as your point of departure, play a harmonic progression in four-voice texture to establish the original key; then modulate to three different foreign key areas—b̄II, vii, and VI—returning to the original key after each modulation. In the last example, use an altered pivot chord or, perhaps, a common tone. Be sure to conclude with a confirming cadence in each new key.

Keyboard Exercises for Chapter 35

1 The following root-position ninth and eleventh chords, denoted by commercial chord symbols, are all based on a common root of E. Transpose each chord to the roots of G, A, D, F, and C. Refer to Appendix 4 of the textbook.

Example K35.1

E^9 $E^{9(\Delta 7)}$ E^{-9} Em^9 E^{11} (omit 3rd) Em^{11} E^{+11}

2 In keys with up to three sharps or flats, approach and resolve a V^9 in a major key and a V^{-9} in a minor key. Use four-voice texture; omit the chordal 5th of the ninth chord.

3 Play the following progressions then transpose them to two other keys of your choice. Identify the chord type of each sonority as you play it.

Example K35.3

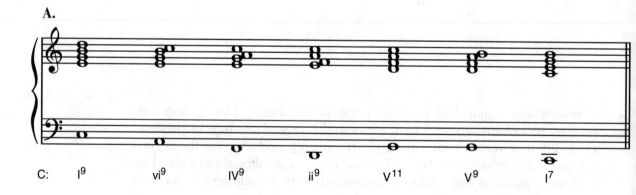

A.

C: I^9 vi^9 IV^9 ii^9 V^{11} V^9 I^7

B.

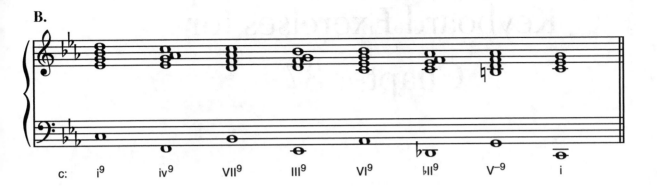

c: i⁹   iv⁹   VII⁹   III⁹   VI⁹   ♭II⁹   V⁻⁹   i

4 Play the indicated chord above the given bass using five-voice texture. Make a smooth soprano line; some notes are suggested. Since this assignment is in jazz style, you need not be concerned with parallels.

Example K35.4

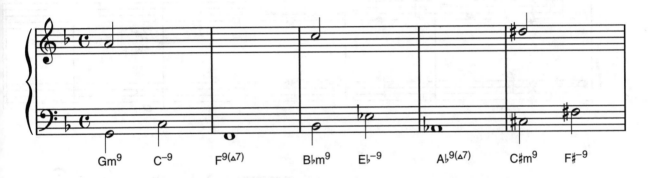

Gm⁹   C⁻⁹   F⁹⁽△⁷⁾   B♭m⁹   E♭⁻⁹   A♭⁹⁽△⁷⁾   C♯m⁹   F♯⁻⁹

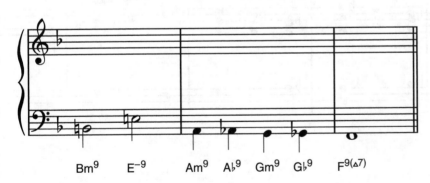

Bm⁹   E⁻⁹   Am⁹   A♭⁹   Gm⁹   G♭⁹   F⁹⁽△⁷⁾

Keyboard Exercises for
Chapter 37

1 Play the three different settings of the descending chromatic tetrachord given below then transpose each one to two other keys of your choice. Identify the type of underlying sequential motion in each.

Example K37.1

A.

B.

C.

2 Realize the following figured-bass examples, which employ various types of chromatic sequences.

Example K37.2

A.

B.

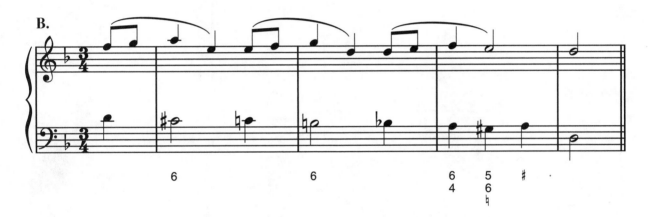

3 Play the beginning of each sequential passage and continue the pattern to the concluding cadences. Transpose these to one other key of your choice. The sequence in Example K37.3A is somewhat free.

Example K37.3

A.

B.

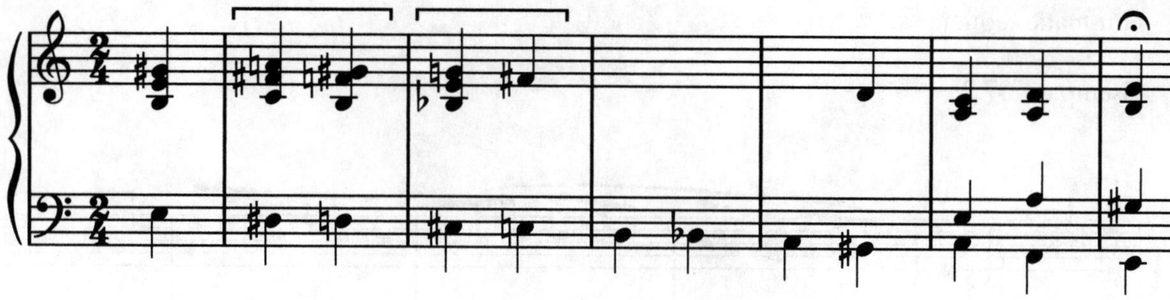

Keyboard Exercises for
Chapter 39

1 Play the following C major pattern (measures 1–2), which employs chromaticism by contrary motion. Then transpose it by successive perfect 5ths, starting with F major. The beginning of each pattern is given. Which harmony is being prolonged in each case?

Example K39.1

2 Play the following passage then transpose it to one other key of your choice. Identify the chromatic voice leading as you play.

Example K39.2

3 Realize the following figured-bass examples in four-voice texture. Cite any examples of chromaticism by contrary motion. The figured-bass symbols are necessarily quite complicated.

Sometimes composers spelled out their names in musical notation. Whose name is spelled by the first four pitches in the bass line of Example K39.3B?

Example K39.3

A.

B.

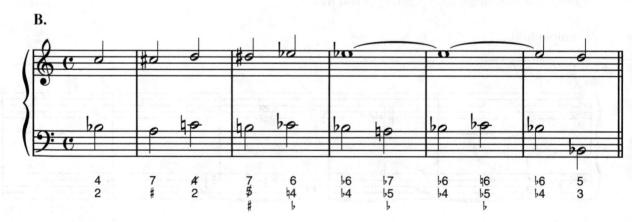

Keyboard Exercises for
Chapter 40

1   Use the diminished seventh chord F♯ A C E♭ in the following passage as a pivot chord, spelled enharmonically if necessary, to modulate from C minor to G minor, B♭ minor, C♯ minor, and E minor. Be sure to conclude with a confirming cadence in the new key.

Example K40.1

c:

2   Using a Ger⁶₅ spelled enharmonically as a V⁷ or vice versa, compose three short chord progressions that modulate from C minor to D♭ major, B minor, and E minor. Be sure to establish both your original key and the new key each time.

3   Continue the following half-step sequence to B♭ major. How is this series of ascending chromatic tonicizations achieved?

Example K40.3

4   The following passages shift to a foreign key by strict sequential modulation. Play the original phrase then follow it with an exact sequential repetition to the indicated key.

Example K40.4

A.

A: ♭VI

B.

E♭:   III

Keyboard Exercises for
Chapter 41

1 Continue the following two sequences in strict fashion. In Example K41.1B, the pattern moves from C major through A♭ and E and back to the original key. What is the function of the even-numbered chords in the first passage?

Example K41.1

A.

B.

2 This passage prolongs a V⁷ through an omnibus progression by descending minor 3rds. Play this progression then transpose it to two other keys of your choice.

Example K41.2

C: (V⁷)   (V⁷)

3   The following example is based on the opening section of the "Liebestod" from
Wagner's *Tristan und Isolde*. Realize the figured bass in the first two measures
then continue the sequence in strict fashion. Which scale is suggested by the
notes indicated with arrows? (Refer to Appendix 2 of the textbook.)

Example K41.3